Juliet Sear

BOTANICAL BAKING

Contemporary baking
and cake decorating with
edible flowers and herbs

www.fwmedia.co.uk

CONTENTS

INTRODUCTION

HELLO AND WELCOME TO BOTANICAL BAKING. THANK YOU FOR CHOOSING MY BOOK!

I'm Juliet and I'm a baker, cake maker and food stylist, among other things. I've been lucky enough to be immersed in the food world, specialising in baking and cake decoration for the last two decades. I've worked with all kinds of decorating techniques and recently the trend for working with edible flowers has really grown (pardon the pun!). For the past few years I've been working with them in my baking to create lots of lovely eye-catching designs.

I'm certainly not claiming to be an expert in edible flowers, but I do love using them to create really pretty cakes and bakes. I'm lucky enough to have a couple of fantastic growers who supply me with edible flowers, and I've been working with the fabulous Jan Billington (a brilliant organic flower farmer) for a few years and also the team at Nurtured in Norfolk. One day maybe I will try and grow my own... In the last few years some supermarkets have also been selling them in their salad selections, which is brilliant!

There are so many wonderful blooms to choose from, and I've been exploring lots of different ways to use them. In the past I'd have made intricate sugar versions of many flowers, but it is lovely to use real flowers. They really are stunning. Not even the most skilful sugarcraft artist can replicate the beauty of a fresh edible flower. And using fresh has the added bonus that nature has done all the work for us – no need to spend hours upon hours creating chocolate or sugar ones!

I love creating modern designs, and really have enjoyed putting this book together. I hope you'll be inspired. For example, using edible flowers to replicate those cool floral structures you might see at events... I've created a version that is a cake topper! There are lots of ways you can preserve and use edible flowers, and in this book I explain how, and suggest good ways to use certain types of preserved flowers, along with fresh.

What I really love about edible flowers is that even the most novice baker can create stunning 'wedding-worthy' designs by creatively placing or decorating with flowers. And if you are time poor, they are the perfect solution too. Edible flowers are easily available to order online from fabulous suppliers, and even some supermarkets. You can always substitute different varieties depending on what's available to you or alter designs to fit your colour scheme. Maybe you'll beat me to it and grow your own!

I've absolutely loved working on this book and really hope you enjoy baking and making the designs, but more importantly, that you are inspired to include edible flowers in your baking.

Please share pictures of any of your bakes – I'd love to see them! Use the hashtag #botanicalbaking and tag me on social media, instagram @julietsear, tweet me at @julietsear_ or find me on facebook @julietsearbakes.

ENJOY!

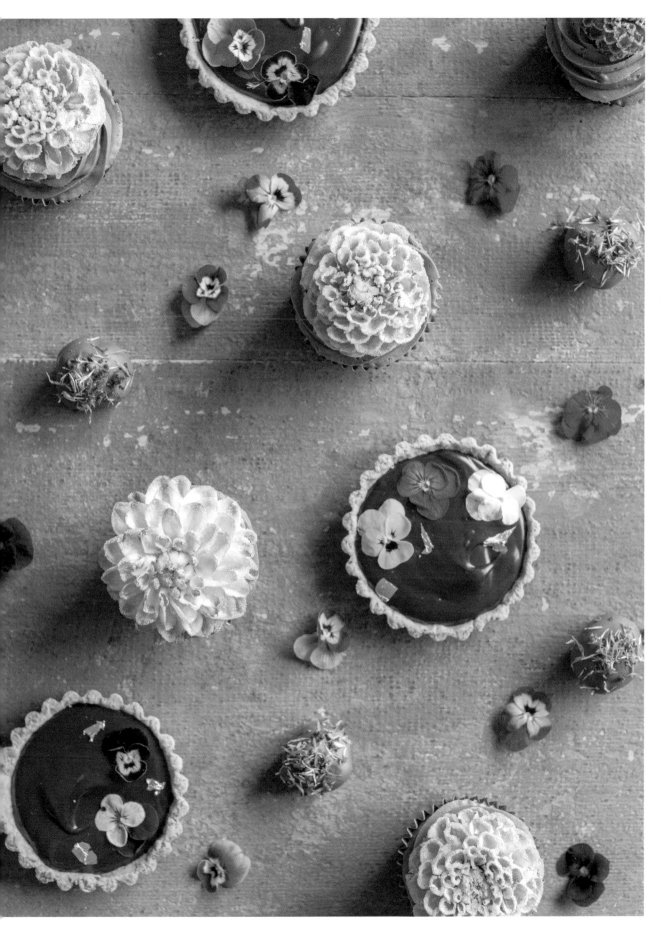

HOW TO USE THIS BOOK

Before you get started, please have a glance through the following points, which explain how this book works and will give you some general advice about how I achieve my results.

» Throughout this book you'll find repeated elements, such as sponges and frostings, that form the base of the individual cakes and bakes. So to save boring you and repeating the recipe each time, I'll refer you back to the Baking Basics section when you're making the later designs.

» In the same way, some decorating steps or techniques apply to several cakes, so for some designs I've given instructions for how to decorate the cake but I've listed the pages you can refer back to for techniques.

I'VE GOT A GOOD TIP IF YOU NEED TO WORK OUT HOW MUCH CAKE MIX YOU NEED: WEIGH YOUR CAKE TIN, ZERO YOUR SCALES WITH THE EMPTY TIN ON THEM, AND THEN FILL THE TIN WITH 4CM (1½IN) OF WATER. THE WEIGHT OF THE TIN AND WATER WILL GIVE YOU A PRETTY GOOD INDICATION OF THE TOTAL CAKE BATTER WEIGHT YOU WILL NEED.

» The idea with the larger cakes is that you can make any size cake you want, so you don't have to stick to the set sizes that I have done. I've given you a guide to the sizes I have used and approximately how many people they would serve. For example, the Electro-pop Drip Cake is a four-tier cake which will serve around 80-100 small portions, but you might want to make a mini version, for example a two-tier.

» When filling cake tins, I like to weigh the batter (see Calculating Cake Batter Quantities on page 22 for a rough guide), but also take a look at the tip on this page to help you work out how much you will need for your particular cake tins.

» All eggs are medium size unless stated. Or in some cases, I suggest weighing beaten egg to be precise.

» All oven temperatures given are for fan ovens.

» Test cakes for 'doneness' with a metal skewer, sharp knife or cake tester; it should come out clean from the centre when the cake is cooked unless the recipe states a cake should be fudgy.

» I suggest using cake drum or boards for each cake tier, but it's a good idea to have additional boards larger than your cakes as it makes crumb coating and icing less messy. In addition, you can easily place your cakes in the fridge to chill, lifting them by the boards so you don't damage them.

» When considering how long your cake will stay fresh, the recipe of the sponge determines the storage time. The preserved flowers last for ages so once the cake is iced and decorated it will keep for as long as your sponge allows.

» Of course you can swap recipes and
use any flavour cake bases that you
like (see Sponge Flavour Switch-ups
on page 22). I think I've got some
yummy recipes in here and I hope
you'll agree, but ultimately my goal
is really about inspiring eye-catching
cake decorating using edible flowers
displayed in different ways. I hope
it will give you ideas and you can
change anything to suit your needs.
I've loved writing this book, and
I hope you are inspired to create
some masterpieces of your own!

ABOUT EDIBLE FLOWERS

I've used many wonderful edible flowers in this book and in the following pages I have suggested ways to choose, store and preserve them so you can create your own selection to use on your cakes and bakes.

I'm incredibly lucky as here in the UK we have so many beautiful edible flowers to choose from, but many of these also grow in other places around the world. If you cannot get hold of certain varieties that I have used in the designs in this book, you can certainly substitute them with others and achieve a similar look.

I do not claim to be an expert on edible flowers, but I have been using them as baking and cake decorations for a few years now and have included many of my favourite ways to use them in this book. As you will see, in some cases, I have used flowers inside the filling or occasionally in part of the bake (see my Flowerfetti Inside Out Cake, on page 92). Edible flowers have been around for centuries, often used in both sweet and savoury cooking, and I think they are the best type of cake decoration you can buy.

SOURCING FLOWERS

You may be lucky enough to be growing your own edible flowers so you will be sure these are safe to eat. I've been given some good advice about edible flowers from my wonderful suppliers, who have some general rules around the use of edible flowers, which are useful to bear in mind.

BE 100% CERTAIN WHAT IT IS

It seems like common sense, but it's definitely worth saying – not all flowers are edible. Don't make the assumption that similar plants are all edible, or even that the whole plant is ok to eat just because part of it is. With some flowers, it's not just that they don't taste pleasant, but they could actually cause you harm. You need to be absolutely certain that what you are proposing to eat (or even more so, what you are proposing to feed to others!) is safe, in order to avoid accidental poisoning.

KNOW WHERE THEY COME FROM

You may be certain of the variety, but don't just welcome any flower into your baking and cake decorating! Garden centres, florists and supermarkets are offering plants that have often been sprayed with insecticides and fungicides to make them perfect to look at but definitely not to eat. Edible flowers will be grown, harvested and handled in the knowledge they will end up as food, unlike those in the florists, so beware. Also don't pick flowers by roadside verges or at low-level near paths used by dog walkers – the first may be contaminated with exhaust pollutants and the second by, shall we say, 'natural doggy by-products'!

THINK ABOUT POLLEN ALLERGIES

Be cautious about eating flowers if you suffer from severe hay fever or any other plant-triggered allergies. Pollen, which most flowers contain, is a well-known allergen. It's wise just to try a little bit the first time you taste a particular flower, and be careful when serving to guests. As a rule to stick to: only eat the petals of flowers, discarding all the other parts before eating. This won't be possible if you're using very tiny flowers such as alyssum though, as you would need a microscope to remove the pistils and stamens successfully!

CONSIDER ORGANIC AND SEASONAL

Buying organic guarantees that your flowers will have been grown in the most natural way possible. If you also choose flowers that are in bloom in the season you are baking in and that have been grown locally, or are even home grown, you will know just what you're getting. Sometimes though, you just have to have a particular bloom, and these are always available from exceptional growers. If you really need something special for your masterpiece you can always do as Michelin-starred chefs do and order a luxury flower wheel from a grower such as Nurtured in Norfolk or choose some incredible organic blooms from Maddocks Farm Organics. It will allow you to create something stunning!

FLOWER FLAVOUR

Flowers vary greatly in terms of taste. Many are mild, delicate and floral, while others can have quite a strong bite to them. You'll find details of each flower's flavour here, and you may decide to use different flowers than I have, according to your taste. Indeed, you may choose to use some flowers simply for decoration and not eat them at all! It's totally up to you – it's down to personal choice.

APPLE BLOSSOM

Flavour: Apple flavour with hints of honeysuckle
Notes: Very pretty as a garnish, or added to jelly
As seen in: Apple Blossom Loaf Cake

CALENDULA

Flavour: sweet and mild, with a warm spicy undertone
Notes: High in vitamins A and C, use for flavour and colour
As seen in: Floral Krispie Cake Topper, Orange and Almond 'Touch of Frosting' Cake, Flowerfetti Inside Out Cake

ALYSSUM

Flavour: Pungent flavour and honey-like fragrance
Notes: Makes a pretty, delicate garnish for fruit, or can be frozen in ice cubes
As seen in: Chouxnuts, Blousy Blooms Bunting Cake, Dried Flowers Watercolour Cake

BELLIS DAISY

Flavour: Mildly bitter
Notes: Use whole, or pull the petals from the flowerheads to make a garnish you can sprinkle
As seen in: Meringue Lollies, Blousy Blooms Bunting Cake, Pressed Flower Faux Frames

CANDYTUFT

Flavour: Rather bitter
Notes: Once used for the treatment of gastric problems
As seen in: Lemon Cookie Monogram Cake

AMARANTH

Flavour: Earthy and nutty
Notes: Often used in savoury dishes, it can complement sweet flavours too
As seen in: Dried Flowers Chocolate Bark, Ganache Trio, Dried Flowers Watercolour Cake

BUTTERFLY SORREL, PINK

Flavour: Mild lemon flavour with a tart background
Notes: Can be added to salad and soups
As seen in: Chouxnuts

CARNATION

Flavour: Slightly clove-like taste, spicy and floral
Notes: Add whole flowers or petals for flavour as well as decoration
As seen in: Lemon Cookie Monogram Cake

CORNFLOWER

Flavour: Very mild peppery aroma, with a hint of sweet spice
Notes: Use whole or combine the petals with other flowers as decorative confetti
As seen in: Iced Rings, Dried Flowers Chocolate Bark, Cupcake Wreath, Ultimate Vegan Choc Cake

DIANTHUS

Flavour: Clove-like flavour, sweet and spicy, somewhat bitter scent
Notes: Great for adding colour and elegance
As seen in: Iced Rings, Ganache Trio, Jelly and Cream Sponge Cake

FUCHSIAS

Flavour: Very mild sweetness with a hint of lemon
Notes: Use the pretty flowers whole
As seen in: Sugar Lollies, Ultimate Vegan Choc Cake, Flowerfetti Inside Out Cake

CUCUMBER FLOWERS

Flavour: Cool and mild with a lovely crunchy texture
Notes: Use fresh for best results
As seen in: Iced Rings

FENNEL

Flavour: Pollen carries a warm aniseed or liquorice taste
Notes: Packed with nutrients including vitamins A, C and B-6
As seen in: Macarons, Pressed Flower Faux Frames

LAVENDER

Flavour: Very fragrant with an instantly recognisable floral aroma
Notes: Use dry or fresh. Can be used to make tea
As seen in: Lavender Biscuits, Flowerfetti Inside Out Cake, Pressed Flower Faux Frames

13

DAHLIA

Flavour: Flavours depend on variety, some are spicy and apple-like, others more like water chestnut
Notes: Wonderful for crystallising, or can be used fresh
As seen in: Cupcake Wreath, Ganache Trio, Faux Flowerpot Illusion Cakes

FIRE FEATHERS (CELOSIA)

Flavour: Neutral, almost flavourless
Notes: Best used as a garnish due to their slightly woody texture
As seen in: Dried Flowers Chocolate Bark, Floral Krispie Cake Topper, Blousy Blooms Bunting Cake

LEMON VERBENA

Flavour: Slightly sour, but with a sweet and fruity flavour that is more potent than other lemon-scented herbs
Notes: Rich in essential oils and commonly used in herbal remedies for digestive ailments, fever and depression
As seen in: Faux Flowerpot Illusion Cakes

MINT, FLOWERING

Flavour: Fresh, distinctive flavour
Notes: Use the flowers and the leaves, both will add a fresh mint flavour
As seen in: Cupcake Wreath, Pistachio, Mint and Yoghurt Cake, Butterfly Wildflower Meadow Cake

OXFORD BLUE TIP (SALVIA HORMINUM)

Flavour: Herbal and slightly spicy
Notes: Use the aromatic leaves and flowering stems to add colour
As seen in: Macarons, Pressed Flower Faux Frames

PRIMROSE

Flavour: Delicate and fragrant
Notes: Perfect as a fresh garnish or set in a jelly
As seen in: Spring Flowers Bundt Cake

ORCHID

Flavour: Depending on type, orchids can be richly vanilla and spice flavoured or subtly sweet and grass-like
Notes: Use fresh as an exotic and stunning decoration
As seen in: Blousy Blooms Bunting Cake

PANSY

Flavour: Slightly sweet lettuce-like flavour and velvety in texture
Notes: The large flat flowers can be floated on jellies, pressed or used fresh
As seen in: Jelly and Cream Sponge Cake, Butterfly Wildflower Meadow Cake

PURPLE SWEET POTATO LEAVES

Flavour: Very slightly bitter when raw
Notes: Can be used like spinach when cooked
As seen in: Bold Botanical Leaf Cake

14

OREGANO FLOWER

Flavour: Spicy, pungent and slightly bitter
Notes: Nutrient rich and flavourful
As seen in: Chouxnuts, Dried Flowers Watercolour Cake

PARADISE FLOWER (ABUTILON)

Flavour: Mildly citrus, a little lettuce-like with a subtle sweetness
Notes: Add a splash of vibrant colour
As seen in: Electro-pop Drip Cake

ROSE

Flavour: Unmistakeable intense floral aroma
Notes: Rich in anti-oxidants, use petals or whole flowers
As seen in: Iced Rings, Rose and Lychee Cake, Brushstrokes and Blooms Cake

ROSEMARY

Flavour: Distinctive, herbal and slightly bitter

Notes: Flowers are blue or mauve, foliage is useful for its robust strength and characterful shape

As seen in: Orange and Almond 'Touch of Frosting' Cake

SUNFLOWER

Flavour: Slightly nutty in flavour

Notes: Use the petals to add bold bright accents

As seen in: Lemon Cookie Monogram Cake

VELVET CORAL (CELOSIA CRISTATA)

Flavour: Very mild, but pleasant

Notes: Considered a foodstuff in its native Africa, exotically shaped for dramatic designs

As seen in: Blousy Blooms Bunting Cake

SAGE, BLACKCURRANT AND PINEAPPLE

Flavour: Decorative and bursting with notes of citrus and mint

Notes: Flowers and leaves can be used. Choose a variety with leaf colour that suits your design

As seen in: Iced Rings, Faux Flowerpot Illusion Cakes, Bold Botanical Leaf Cake

SWEET CICELY

Flavour: Sweet anise flavour

Notes: Pretty and frothy to add a delicate element to a design

As seen in: Cupcake Wreath, Faux Flowerpot Illusion Cakes, Butterfly Wildflower Meadow Cake

VIOLA

Flavour: Slightly sweet flavour and delightful velvety texture

Notes: Smaller and more delicate than a pansy with purple, violet and yellow shades most common

As seen in: Macarons, Ganache Trio, Gin and Tonic Cake Tails

SNAPDRAGON

Flavour: Almost flavourless, perhaps a slight bitterness

Notes: Great for adding colour, characterful shaped flowers

As seen in: Iced Rings, Macarons, Floral Krispie Cake Topper

TAGETES

Flavour: Citrus flavour

Notes: Species come in a variety of sizes and add a bright pop of colour

As seen in: Meringue Lollies, Cupcake Wreath, Buttercream Cactus Garden Cake, Lemon Cookie Monogram Cake

ZINNIA

Flavour: Rather bitter

Notes: Use petals as confetti or whole flowers for punchy colour

As seen in: Cupcake Wreath, Pistachio, Mint and Yoghurt Cake

STORING AND PRESERVING

There are a variety of ways to prepare edible flowers which will allow you to use them in many different aspects of baking, and also helps to preserve them so they are available when you need them, rather than just when they are seasonally in flower. A classic example is when I make elderflower syrup in June, so I can use it for the rest of the year. Once you have picked edible flowers, keep them in the fridge until you are ready either to use them fresh on a cake, or preserve them. A good tip is to sit them on a little piece of kitchen paper that has been dampened with water, this helps to keep them fresh. They need to be kept like this as otherwise they will die very quickly.

FLORAL SYRUPS

These are lovely to drizzle onto sponges or add to toppings or fillings – I've used elderflower in the Jelly and Cream Sponge Cake on page 76, for example. You can use a range of flowers to make delicious syrups, including lavender, rose, hibiscus and violets, and also many herbs, so just experiment to see what you like.

ELDERFLOWER CORDIAL RECIPE

Elderflower is so abundant in our gardens in the UK, but when its season is over it's gone. However, you can bottle its delicious floral flavour for use all year round with this syrup. It lasts for a couple of months in the fridge, and can be frozen in ice cube trays or food bags and defrosted as needed.

Ingredients

2.25kg (5lb) white caster (superfine) sugar

2 large unwaxed lemons, zest pared and fruit sliced

20-24 fresh elderflower heads, stalks removed

80g (2¾oz) citric acid

Method

1. Shake off the elderflowers to get rid of any debris or little bugs, then swish them around in a large bowl or bucket of clean water, lift out and shake off the excess water.

2. Put the sugar and 1.5ltrs (2¾ pints) water into a large saucepan and heat gently until the sugar granules are all dissolved, stirring occasionally. Once the sugar has completely dissolved, bring the pan of syrup to the boil and let it bubble for a minute, then turn off the heat.

3. Add the elderflower heads, lemon zest and slices and citric acid to the syrup and stir well. Cover the pan and leave to infuse for 24 hours, stirring halfway through that time.

4. Strain through a muslin or clean tea towel. Use a funnel or ladle to fill sterilised bottles. Chill or freeze as needed.

SUSPENDING IN SUGAR

I've found that melting down clear mints and adding edible flowers works really well. I've done this to make my Sugar Lollies on page 46. Once encapsulated in the sweets, the flowers will last well for a couple of weeks, suspended in sugary time.

CRYSTALLISING EDIBLE FLOWERS

Crystallising is a pretty way to preserve flowers - they are a sweet crisp sugar-coated treat.

There are a few ways you can do this and most flowers can be crystallised, though some are more fiddly than others. For example very tiny soft delicate petals are trickier than simple large rose petals, it just takes time and patience. The most important thing is to ensure you coat all of the petals completely, so you may have to wiggle the brush in between petals. I used this method for the preserved dahlias in this book, it took a while but the effect was really beautiful. They looked lovely as giant pom pom decorations for my Ganache Cupcakes on page 54.

The most common method is to use egg white and sugar. Once preserved like this, the flowers will certainly keep for a few weeks, and depending on the variety, crystallised flowers can last for many months if you substitute the egg for Gum Arabic (see below) and store them in a cake box layered between paper and kept out of sunlight, in a cool, dry place.

VEGAN-FRIENDLY CRYSTALLISING

For a longer life you can use food grade Gum Arabic to adhere the sugar to the flowers. With egg white the crystallised flowers will last a couple of weeks, but with Gum Arabic they will store for several weeks or in some cases months. Gum Arabic can be bought online or ordered in from a good chemist. A small pot is not expensive and lasts for ages. To use this, dilute a couple of teaspoons of Gum Arabic into a flavourless alcohol such as vodka until you have a consistency slightly thinner than single cream. The Gum Arabic will need to be left to sit in the alcohol overnight to ensure that it properly dissolves. This is also a good method if you are making a cake for vegans or anyone with an egg allergy. I have also used chickpea water (aqua faba) for crystallising flowers and it worked extremely well. Treat it in the same way you would egg white. It's a little thinner but it works and is perfect for vegans.

A
B

Method

1. Fine white caster (superfine) sugar is best for crystallising. Using a soft, fine paintbrush, gently paint either with egg white, aqua faba or Gum Arabic liquid onto the edible flowers (on both sides of the petals).

2. Then sprinkle the sugar carefully all over them - on both sides and in the cracks and crevices - so that it adheres. Knock off any surplus sugar and place on a baking sheet, lined with baking parchment, to dry. If you get too much sugar stuck to the petals, the flowers can get pulled out of shape and flattened, so this process may take a bit of practice.

3. Depending on the temperature in the room, the flowers may take a few hours to dry and should then be kept in an airtight container until use. The colour can also fade from the flowers if they are kept in direct sunlight, so store them carefully.

PRESSING EDIBLE FLOWERS AND LEAVES

Pressing edible flowers is the same as pressing any flowers. It is simple to do. I use a flower press because I like to do a lot! Presses are inexpensive, but you can of course stick to the old-fashioned method of using heavy books. Remember that it's important to have good paper to press with, blotting paper is best.

To get the best results press the flowers when they are as fresh as possible. Pick blossoms and petals that haven't been bruised, torn, damaged, or wilted. If they have a thick stem part at the back of the flower, try and cut this down as much as you can without going so far that the flower breaks apart.

Flowers with naturally flat faces, such as pansies or violas, are easier to press than flowers that have more three-dimensional shape like orchids, whole roses, or dahlias. But as long as you place them carefully and are sure to tighten the flower press regularly, smaller roses work well (see Pressed Flower Faux Frames, page 122, the red roses are so pretty). Of course, you can take edible flowers apart to press them; I love pressing rose petals. Some edible flowers have more moisture, like the little daisies, which have quite juicy centres, they just may take a little more time. I press my edible flowers for a minimum of a week, although some of the more succulent ones, including the roses and daisies, may take longer.

Many leaves such as sweet cicely are lovely when pressed, although some just go a bit crisp, so it's always worth experimenting to see what works for you. Whole lavender stems, flowering herbs and fennel came out really well. See my Macarons on page 38 – the small yellow roses are really lovely, but there's no denying that if you want a pressed flower that's looks very like the fresh flower, violas and pansies do have the best look. I love the vintage effect you get from pressed flowers and they will keep for months as long as you are careful to keep them out of direct sunlight and completely dry.

Method

1. Unscrew the flower press and take off the top piece of wood. Place one piece of cardboard on the bottom of the press (you can use any thin cardboard, you can even recycle packaging as long as it is plain, not printed), and place one sheet of flower press paper (or blotting paper) on top of the cardboard.

2. Arrange your flowers on the flower press paper, taking care to have them as flat as you can so that when pressed they look open.

3. Add a second piece of paper over the top of your flowers, then add more cardboard, taking care not to move anything.

4. You can repeat this process and build up several layers depending on the size of the flowers and how big your press is. Once full replace the top piece of wood and screw the wingnuts as tightly as you can.

5. Make sure you tighten the screws daily. If your press is large you can even stand on it to add pressure when doing this, or just use your hand, or something like a heavy pestle and mortar, to push down as much as you can and tighten. Store in a dry place in your house, I keep mine in the airing cupboard as it's dark and dry.

6. When your flowers are pressed, they will be very delicate so handle them with care... sometimes it's useful to use tweezers to lift and place them if they are absolutely paper thin, it depends on the type.

Alternatively you can use heavy books to press your flowers, make sure you don't mind if they get a bit wrinkly or damaged though! Use blotting paper in the same way and use extra weight on top of the books to aid the pressing process. Take care to leave quite a few pages in between layers (if you are pressing more than one layer of flowers at once) as sometimes the moisture might cause some mould.

Some people rate 'pressing' flowers in a microwave, and you can find instructions for this online, however I don't like this method as I think they lose a bit of their colour.

DRYING EDIBLE FLOWERS

Some flowers dry better than others – I love dried fire feathers and oregano flowers – but all flowers will dry. Some work better for using as flowerfetti, as you can easily crumble them up once dry, see the Dried Flowers Chocolate Bark on page 48. If you wish a whole flower to stay intact (for example a viola or pansy), be sure to lay it carefully, with the open face facing downwards and the petals arranged flat so they don't fold over.

Method

1. I find the best way to dry flowers is simply to arrange a few sheets of kitchen paper onto trays and lay out the flowers so they are not overlapping or covering each other.

2. Leave the flowers out to air in a dry dark place, and they will dry out well after a few days.

3. Once they have finished drying I find the best way to store the flowers is inside cake box lids, with some kitchen paper in between layers so they are kept away from light. They will last for many months as long as they're stored properly.

I have used a dehydrator for drying flowers, but I find this rushed process doesn't give as pretty a finish and some of the flower petals frizzle up more than when dried by the longer natural method.

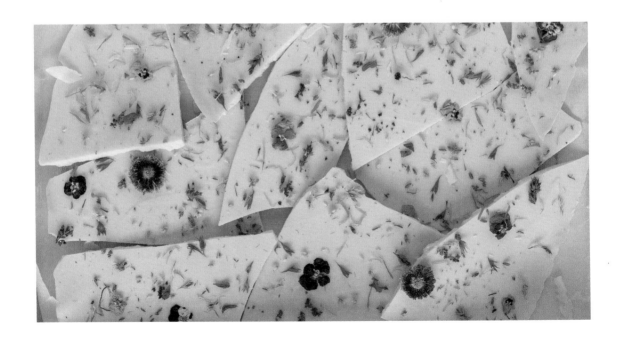

BAKING BASICS

To avoid repeating the recipes that I use regularly for the cakes in this book, and to keep all the cake construction techniques in one handy reference section, I've gathered all the basic instructions here. You're welcome!

VERY VANILLA SPONGE RECIPE

This simple sponge recipe, I like to call my very vanilla recipe as I always put lots of vanilla bean paste into the batter. This mixture can be used to make layer cakes - many of the multi-tier cakes in this book are created using this basic sponge - as well as cupcakes like the ones in the Cupcake Wreath on page 50.

You can add additional flavourings to this basic recipe, as suggested in many of the cake recipes. For example, I use this recipe for the Flowerfetti Inside Out Cake on page 92, and added a mix of edible flowers including fresh lavender to give the sponge a herby lavender taste.

CALCULATING CAKE BATTER QUANTITIES

I've suggested sizes and layer numbers for making the cakes in this book, but of course you could adapt any of the instructions to make larger cakes or more tiers by just increasing the batter amount as needed. I prefer to weigh my cake batter into the tins to keep all the layers equal heights. A top tip for working out a guide as to how much total batter weight you will need, is to fill each tin with water to a 4cm (1½in) height and total up how much is needed. For example, my Flowerfetti cake is made up of two tiers - 10cm (4in) and 18cm (7in) round cakes - and each tier is made with two layers of sponge. Therefore the batter weight to add to each tin is 175g for each 10cm (4in) layer, and 375g batter in each 18cm (7in) layer. The total weight of cake batter is 1.1kg (2lb 6oz), so make a 6 egg mix using the Very Vanilla Sponge Recipe, and you'll have a tiny bit left over. If you need a lot of batter for one of the larger cakes, you can multiply the quantities. For example, the four-tier Electro-pop Drip Cake on page 134 requires 4.7kg (10lb 4oz) of sponge batter. In that case, make two and a half times the amount in the recipe below by multiplying all the ingredients weights by 2.5, so make a 15 egg mix. I often make a few cupcakes and pop them in the oven with the main cake if I have spare batter.

Makes 1.2kg (2lb 10½oz) batter

Ingredients

300g (10½oz) soft salted butter, at room temperature, plus extra for greasing

300g (10½oz) golden caster (superfine) sugar

2 tsp vanilla bean paste, I love using the Nielsen-Massey vanilla bean paste as it is the most natural flavour and is alcohol free, or flavourings of your choice (see below)

6 medium free-range eggs, lightly beaten

300g (10½oz) self-raising (-rising) flour with 1 tsp baking powder lightly whisked through

Method

1. Place the butter, sugar and vanilla (or other flavourings if using) into a large bowl or your mixer bowl and combine.

2. Turn the mixer speed to high (or if you're using a wooden spoon, use plenty of elbow grease!) and beat until the mixture is very pale, soft and fluffy and the granules of sugar have disappeared.

3. Add the egg, about one quarter at a time, beating it in.

4. Add the flour gradually, one quarter at a time, mixing gently on a slow speed, until it has been incorporated. Fold with a metal spoon if doing this by hand. Take care not to mix or beat vigorously or your sponge can turn out a bit tough.

5. For cupcakes bake for around 12 minutes, checking every few minutes, or see the baking time given in the recipe for larger cakes. Cakes should be a light golden brown, springy to the touch when they are cooked. A sharp knife, cake tester or metal skewer should come out clean and free of mixture.

SPONGE FLAVOUR SWITCH-UPS

For a different sponge flavour try adding one of the following: **Lemon or orange** - add zest of two lemons, or zest of one large orange; **brown sugar/caramel** - switch the sugar for light muscovado for a deeper caramel taste; **chocolate** - switch 30g (1oz) flour for cocoa powder (unsweetened cocoa) and add an extra ½ tsp baking powder to the dry ingredients.

VANILLA BUTTERCREAM

I use this buttercream recipe for all my basic frosting, and as the base for my chocolate ganache buttercream. You can vary the flavour by adding lemon zest or flower syrups, or stirring in edible flowers. Bear in mind that some flavours may add colour too (lemon can make the buttercream somewhat yellow), so consider whether you want that effect or not when choosing to add anything to the basic recipe.

Just as with calculating cake batter quantities (see box on page 22), if you need more than the 1.5kg (3lb 5oz) of buttercream that this recipe makes, just multiply all the amounts. It's worth making more than you need because running out before your cake is fully covered is something of a nightmare, so err on the side of generous when calculating amounts.

Makes 1.5kg (3lb 5oz) buttercream

Ingredients

500g (1lb 2oz) soft unsalted butter

1kg (2lb 4oz) icing (confectioner's) sugar

2 tsp vanilla bean paste, my preference is the Nielsen-Massey one, or substitute with other flavourings

A few tablespoons of just-boiled water (optional)

Method

1. Place all the ingredients into a large bowl, or the bowl of your mixer. I use Silver Spoon icing sugar as there is no need to sift, but some other icing sugars may need sifting into the bowl to avoid lumps.

2. Set your mixer on a low speed, otherwise you will dust your entire kitchen in powdery icing sugar! Beat the ingredients together until they are pale and smooth. At this point you can add a little just-boiled water, a tablespoon or so at a time, on a low speed and then raise the speed to high. This helps to make the icing paler and more creamy.

PREPARING A CAKE

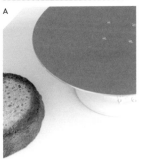

LAYERING AND FILLING

You may require multiple layers of cake per tier depending on the design. These instructions are for creating a tier made of two cakes, one of which is split, filled and layered, thus creating three sponge layers. Of course, you can repeat the steps as needed to make a taller cake, like the Brushstrokes and Blooms Cake on page 118, which has five layers.

Method

1. Generally, sponge cakes will come out of the tin with a slight rounded hump. Trim off the hump from the top of each sponge to level it (A). Slice one of the layers in half through the middle, using a cake leveller or a sharp serrated knife, such as a bread knife.

2. Place a cake drum the same size as the tier you are working on onto a cake turntable on an additional larger cake board. I add a little buttercream between these as then once I've done the crumb coat (see page 26), it is much easier for me to do a second coat of buttercream as the cake will stick in the middle of the board and not move around when you press a palette knife onto the side. Place half of the tier you've cut onto the drum, sticking on with a little buttercream.

3. Spread the sponge with jam (jelly) or curd if using (B), then spread a generous layer of buttercream over the sponge. Top with the other half of the cake layer.

4. Add more buttercream to the top (C), spread jam over the last layer, invert the cut side onto the buttercream (so you have the nice flat part that was in the bottom of the tin to give a neat top), add this final cake layer, push down and check that the layers are in line and level (D).

CRUMB COATING

A crumb coat helps to fill any gaps, seal in the crumbs and begin to create a neat finish.

Method

1. Spread a generous layer of buttercream all around the sides of the tier (A). Cover the top with buttercream too (B). Try to keep your palette knife level so the edges and top are nice and straight.

2. Neaten this layer by holding a side scraper or palette knife against the side of the sponge (C). Press it firmly and straight against the edge of the cake, and scrape the excess buttercream off the sponge, leaving a thin and neat base layer (D).

3. Scrape over the top, and remove any little excess bits of buttercream using a small sharp knife. The aim is to get your crumb coat as neat as possible, and this will make any further coatings much easier and neater.

4. Place the cake in the fridge for about an hour to set nice and firm so that your next layer of decoration will be easy to apply without the sponge layers sliding around.

SECOND COATING WITH BUTTERCREAM

This second coat should be all you need to do, especially for a drip cake or cake with lots of decorations that will be stuck on to the surface. With a highly decorated cake, any odd part that may have a tiny bit of sponge showing can be covered with chocolate, flowers or any other decorative items. Be generous with the second coat of buttercream, it can be a few millimetres (⅛in) thick. Do not use a side scraper yet if you are adding additional colouring like the ombre effect on the Electro-pop Drip Cake on page 134, or the watercolour effect on the Dried Flowers Watercolour Cake on page 130, as you will add the colours first, then scape the surface in one process.

Method

1. In the same way that you added the crumb coat layer, add more buttercream to the sides and top of the cake with a palette knife (E, F and G).

2. Smooth around and scrape off as you did before using a side scraper or palette knife, to give each cake a clean and neat base of buttercream (H).

3. If you wish your cake to have a plain base of frosting that will be quite visible, for example if you are creating the Bold Botanical Leaf Cake on page 116 or the Blousy Blooms Bunting Cake on page 126, use the scraper to neaten off the second coating as carefully as possible at this stage, so that you have a perfect flat base cake ready to decorate.

COVERING WITH SUGARPASTE OR MARZIPAN

Some cake designs work better if coated with sugarpaste, for example cakes that may be painted or have sugar decorations or flowers glued on, such as the Butterfly Wildflower Meadow Cake on page 108, and the Pressed Flower Faux Frames on page 122. You can cover a cake in marzipan first, then add a layer of sugarpaste; this will give you a very flat and neat surface. Some people do not like marzipan or may have a nut allergy, so you can simply coat with one or two layers of sugarpaste. It's entirely down to preference, and of course how much time you wish to spend on covering a cake. Sugarpaste is also referred to as ready-to-roll icing, regalice or fondant.

These instructions work for both marzipan and sugarpaste. If you wish to do a double layer, repeat the process, but rather than using jam (jelly) for the second coating, add a little vodka, brandy or cooled boiled water to the first coating once it has set, in order to dampen it for its second covering.

The table below is a guide to how much sugarpaste or marzipan you might need to cover different sizes of cake. Please think of it only as a rough guide as cake tier heights vary and a taller cake tier will need more sugarpaste. When in doubt, roll out more than you think you need, you can always trim off the excess.

Round cakes, diameter	Sugarpaste required
10cm (4in)	450g (1lb)
12.5cm (5in)	575g (1lb 4½oz)
15cm (6in)	600g (1lb 5oz)
18cm (7in)	750g (1lb 10oz)
20cm (8in)	850g (1lb 14oz)
23cm (9in)	1kg (2lb 4oz)
25cm (10in)	1.2kg (2lb 10½oz)
30cm (12in)	1.6kg (3lb 8oz)

Method

1. Begin with a chilled and crumb coated cake (see page 26). Add a little water to some apricot jam (jelly) and boil it in a saucepan, then brush over the cake and cake drum to make the whole thing sticky.

2. Knead enough marzipan or sugarpaste to cover the entire cake, making sure you have plenty to cover the top and sides with a little extra. You may add food colouring at this stage if you need to.

3. Dust your work surface with icing (confectioner's) sugar and then, using guide sticks (if you have them), roll out the sugarpaste or marzipan to just large enough to cover the top and sides of the cake (A). Make sure you give it a quarter turn every so often adding more icing sugar if needed so it does not stick to the surface. You can also smooth the surface with a cake smoother (B).

GUIDE STICKS ARE OPTIONAL, BUT IF YOU DO NOT HAVE ANY BE CAREFUL TO KEEP THE THICKNESS OF THE SUGARPASTE OR MARZIPAN EVEN.

4. Dust a little more icing sugar over the top of the sugarpaste or marzipan, roll it over the pin (C) and lift it up to the cake, making sure you have enough to cover the side facing you and that it is central. Roll the sugarpaste or marzipan away from yourself across the top of the cake and allow it to fall over the far side, avoiding trapping any air (D).

5. Using your hands, smooth the sugarpaste or marzipan gently all over the top and sides of the cake including the drum, avoiding finger marks (E). If you notice any air bubbles use a pin tool, a scriber needle or a clean sewing needle to pop them and gently push the air out.

6. Trim the excess and set it aside (F). It keeps for weeks if it's wrapped in a plastic bag and kept completely airtight.

7. Lift up the cake, place your palm under the cake drum for support and use a smoother to press the sugarpaste or marzipan against the cake and to hang below the drum (G). If you find it hard to lift the cake up in this way, you can place it on something smaller than the drum, such as a can of food or small cake tin to lift the cake up high enough to trim.

8. Using a sharp knife, cut around the base at a flat angle using the drum as a guide to trim neatly so the sugarpaste or marzipan is flush to the bottom of the cake drum (H).

9. Place the cake onto a larger cake board or drum and work with the cake smoothers over the top and sides of the cake, pushing the suagarpaste or marzipan flat onto the cake (I). Make sure you keep the angle of the sides nice and straight, and the top very level so you end up with a neat coating with the top and sides as straight as possible. Leave to dry/set overnight before decorating or stacking together the cake tiers. If you wish to get a very flat and neat coating, you can double ice the cake as mentioned above.

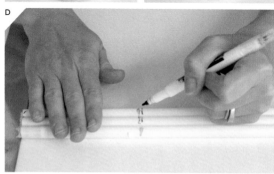

ADDING DOWELS AND STACKING

With stacked cakes, whether they are sugarpaste covered or buttercream coated, support dowels are added to the lower cake tiers to prevent the cakes from collapsing. It sounds tricky but it's really straight forward - do not be afraid! The larger the cakes, the more cake dowels you will need.

Method

1. As a guide it is a good idea to place a spare cake drum on top of the sponge that you are dowelling, the same size as the cake that will be sat on top, then you can use a cocktail stick (toothpick) or scriber needle to mark a circle around the area where you need to place the cake dowels (A).

2. Push the dowels into the cake making sure you have got them nice and straight (B). Position them roughly equally spaced in a ring just within your guide circle, then a few in the centre. On a 30cm (12in) cake I'd recommend using about eight or nine dowels, for a 20cm (8in) cake use five or six dowels, and for a 15cm (6in) that will just have a 10cm (4in) cake on top, you can just use three.

3. Use an edible-ink pen to mark the point where the dowel comes out at the top of the sponge (C).

4. Remove the dowels and line them up next to each other against a straight edge, you need to do this because the marks will slightly vary. No matter how level your cake is there will always be tiny differences in height on the top surface, so mark all of the dowels to the length of the tallest one, so that the cake will be level once stacked (D).

5. Trim the excess from the dowels (save any pieces long enough to use again). Depending on the type of dowels, you may use scissors (E) or for solid ones a hacksaw might be needed.

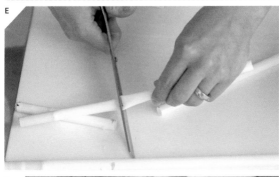

E

F

G

6. Place the dowels back into the cake tier (F). Sometimes, it may be better to get the cakes doweled to this stage, take them to the venue separately, then stack them up on site, rather than travel with a fully stacked cake. Most venues will accommodate you if you need to melt any chocolate or add fresh flowers or decoration on site. It is less worrying to set up a large cake like this in situ unless you are used to transporting tall cakes all the time and don't have far to take it (or many hills or bumpy roads to travel on!).

7. Place the largest base cake onto your serving plate or stand, or cake board.

8. Add additional buttercream or royal icing over the area that you have doweled; if there is any great difference in the heights of the dowels, you may have some gaps in between the tiers, so be sure to save any buttercream to fill them in.

IT'S IMPORTANT IF YOU'RE MAKING THE ELECTRO-POP DRIP CAKE ON PAGE 134 TO SAVE THE COLOURED BUTTERCREAM FOR THE OMBRE EFFECT, JUST IN CASE YOU HAVE A LARGE GAP TO COVER. I WOULD USUALLY JUST ADD A DECORATION OVER A GAP. SOME DESIGNS NEED A CLEANER FINISH SO JUST TAKE THAT INTO CONSIDERATION.

9. Carefully lift the next tier up using a palette knife, line it up over the base tier making sure you are as central as you can be, then place the cake onto the one below. It is a good idea to choose the best looking side of the cake and just use the palette knife at the back of the cake. That way any knocks will not show on the side you have chosen as the front to your cake. If you have any gaps you can fill these with buttercream from a piping bag or palette knife and smooth around to neaten. Repeat for the rest of the tiers until your cake is fully stacked (G).

SWEET
TREATS

LAVENDER
BISCUITS

I love these delicate biscuits, perfect for a special teatime treat or as gifts and party favours. The flavour is divine and adding a little purple colouring to the sugar edge really enhances their appeal. Fresh edible violas are added at the end of the bake with egg white to create a biscuit that's as pretty as a picture.

A  B  C  D

Makes 25–30 biscuits

Prep time, 30 minutes

Chill time, approx 2 hours

Bake time, 25 minutes

Ingredients

250g (8¾oz) white caster (superfine) sugar

15g (½oz) dried lavender

250g (9oz) unsalted butter

1 tsp vanilla bean paste, I used the Nielsen-Massey one

360g (12¾oz) plain (all-purpose) flour

Purple food colouring dust, I've used Sugarflair Aubergine

1 egg white

Edible violas in a variety of colours, I've used purples

Equipment

Cling film (plastic wrap)

Sharp knife

Small paintbrush

Method

1. To make the lavender sugar, blitz the caster sugar and lavender in a food processor until the lavender has been dispersed into a fine dust.

2. Cream together the butter and lavender sugar with the vanilla bean paste until it is pale and fluffy.

3. Add the flour and combine into a soft dough.

4. Split the dough in half and roll each amount into a thick sausage shape with a diameter of around 5cm (2in). Wrap in cling film (plastic wrap) and chill for a couple of hours.

> YOU CAN CHILL THE DOUGH IN THE FRIDGE FOR UP TO TWO DAYS AT THIS STAGE, OR YOU CAN FREEZE IT FOR UP TO A MONTH.

5. Unwrap the chilled dough and cut into 1cm (⅜in) thick slices (A).

6. Add purple food colouring dust to the remaining lavender sugar until you have a lilac coloured sugar (B).

7. Roll the edge of each slice of dough in the coloured lavender sugar (C).

8. Place the biscuits on a lined baking tray and bake at 180°C (350°F) for 15 minutes.

9. Remove the biscuits from the oven, brush the tops with a little egg white and add the violas by pushing them gently into the centre of each warm biscuit. Brush over the top with another layer of egg white to seal the flowers in place (D).

10. Continue baking the biscuits for another 5–10 minutes until the edges turn golden brown.

11. Remove from the oven and leave to cool on a wire rack.

> THESE BISCUITS WILL LAST FOR UP TO TWO WEEKS IF KEPT WELL WRAPPED.

ICED RINGS

These beautiful biscuits are both delicious and eye-catching, with the crystallised flowers adding a floral crunch. Perfect for presents, parties or afternoon tea, the recipe is really simple and can be made in various different flavours. The dough rolls out easily and holds its shape, so is ideal for cutting out delicate rings.

A

B

C

D

Makes 16–20 biscuits

Prep time, 1 hour, plus crystallising time (see page 17)

Bake time, 12–15 minutes

Ingredients

200g (7oz) golden caster (superfine) sugar

200g (7oz) salted butter, at room temperature

1 tsp vanilla bean paste

1 medium egg

375g (13¼oz) plain (all-purpose) flour, plus extra for dusting

250g (9oz) royal icing sugar

3–4 tsp water

Variety of crystallised flowers, I've used violas, calendulas, lavender, dianthus, roses, cornflowers, blackcurrant sage, cucumber flowers and snapdragons

Equipment

Fluted circle cutters, 4cm (1½in) and 10cm (4in)

Piping bag

Method

1. Mix the caster sugar, butter and vanilla bean paste until just combined.

2. Gently beat in the egg until fully combined.

3. Add the flour and combine into a dough.

4. Dust the surface with additional flour and roll out to a thickness of 4–5mm (⅛–¼in), turning the dough and adding extra dusting flour as required.

5. Use a 10cm (4in) fluted circle cutter to cut out round biscuits. Cut 4cm (1½in) fluted circles from the centre of each biscuit to create rings (A). Roll out the excess dough and cut out more rings.

6. Place the biscuits on a lined baking tray and bake at 180°C (356°F) for 12–15 minutes until golden.

PRESS YOUR FINGER LIGHTLY ONTO ONE OF THE RINGS. IF THE DOUGH SPRINGS STRAIGHT BACK THEY ARE COOKED, BUT IF AN INDENTATION IS LEFT THEN THEY NEED TO BE BAKED FOR LONGER UNTIL CRISP.

7. Remove from the oven and leave to cool on the tray or on a wire rack.

8. Mix the royal icing sugar with water until it reaches a thick but still runny consistency. The consistency is right when you lift up or drag a spoon through the icing and the trail disappears after 5–10 seconds.

9. Place the icing into a piping bag and pipe a wavy line around the outer edge (B). Pipe a wavy line around the central hole and then fill in the space between the two lines by flooding with icing (C).

IF YOU WANT A QUICKER FINISH, YOU CAN DIP THE RINGS INTO A BOWL OF ICING TO ROUGHLY COVER THE TOP.

10. Place crystallised flowers onto the iced rings to decorate (D). Leave to dry on a wire rack.

MACARONS

Explore your decadent side with these darkly delicious macarons, which combine the rich flavours of chocolate and blackcurrant. You can't beat pansies and violas for pressing, the results are always beautiful, but I've also used fennel, which will add a wonderful aniseed flavour, and a variety of other flowers to decorate.

Makes 20–24 shells

Prep time, 1 hour, plus drying time

Bake time, 15 minutes

Ingredients

150g (5½oz) ground almonds

10g (¼oz) blackcurrant powder

160g (5¾oz) icing (confectioner's) sugar

120ml (4⅛fl oz) egg white

1 tsp vanilla paste

150g (5½oz) caster (superfine) sugar

60ml (2¼fl oz) water

Purple food colouring (optional)

100g (3½oz) blackcurrant jam (jelly)

300g (10½oz) dark (bittersweet) chocolate

150ml (5½fl oz) double (heavy) cream

1 egg white for brushing, or 30ml (1fl oz) pasteurised egg white from a carton (I use 2 Chicks), or 30ml (1fl oz) agave syrup

Pressed flowers of your choice, I've used small roses, fuchsias, fennel, pansies, violas, snapdragons, fire feathers and Oxford blue tips

Equipment

Baking parchment

Baking tray(s)

Piping bag, with a large round 1cm (½in) nozzle

Food processor or bullet blender

Sieve

Stand mixer or electric hand whisk

Saucepan

Sugar thermometer

Method

1. Preheat the oven to 170°C (335°F). Print off a macaron template (see Templates, page 138) if you can (or you can pipe them by eye but it makes them neater if you use a template), and place it under a piece of baking parchment on a baking tray ready to pipe your macarons.

2. Place the ground almonds, blackcurrant powder and icing sugar into a food processor and pulse until really fine. Sieve the mixture to remove any large pieces of almond left behind.

3. Place the almond mixture into a bowl and add half the egg white to form a paste (add a drop of purple food colouring now if you wish to boost the lilac colour).

4. Place the remaining egg white into a clean bowl (a stand mixer is easiest for this but a hand whisk will work too).

>>>>

5. Place the caster sugar and water into a small pan and bring to the boil. Once the sugar starts to bubble and the temperature is approximately 100°C (210°F) start to whisk the egg whites to stiff peaks.

6. Once the sugar syrup reaches 115°C (240°F), slowly pour it into the egg white whilst whisking at a medium speed until all the syrup is incorporated. Continue whisking for 5-10 minutes until the egg white has thickened and gone glossy.

7. Add a spoonful of the meringue mix to the almond mix to loosen it and then use a spatula to fold in the rest of the meringue.

8. Pour the resulting macaron mixture into a piping bag with a round nozzle and carefully pipe onto your tray following the template circles (A).

9. Once you have piped the entire tray of macarons bang the tray firmly onto the surface to get rid of any air bubbles. Leave the macarons to skin over for 25-35 minutes before baking.

10. Bake for 7 minutes, and then open the oven to release the steam. Close the door and continue baking for another 7-8 minutes. Once baked, leave to cool in the trays on top of a wire rack.

11. Brush a little egg white onto half of the macaron shells (these will be the tops) and stick on your chosen pressed flowers. Brush over the flowers with additional egg white if you need to aid sticking. It is best to do this when the macarons are still warm as it helps to dry out the egg white (B and C).

IF YOU'D RATHER NOT USE EGG WHITE OR YOU CAN'T GET THE UNPASTEURISED ONE IN A CARTON, YOU CAN STICK THE PRESSED FLOWERS ONTO THE COOLED MACARONS WITH A TOUCH OF AGAVE SYRUP

12. While the shells are cooling down make the chocolate ganache by heating the cream until just boiling and then pouring it over the chopped chocolate. Mix well until the chocolate has melted into the cream and leave to cool for 20-30 minutes until it is a pipe-able consistency.

13. Once everything is ready, place the ganache into a piping bag and pipe a ring of ganache around the edge of the plain shell (D) and add a little splodge of the jam from a small spoon to fill the centre (E).

14. Pop on a floral shell and gently press down until the filling is pushed out to the edge (F).

IF YOU ARE NOT EATING THE MACARONS STRAIGHT AWAY, THEY CAN BE STORED IN THE FRIDGE FOR UP TO THREE DAYS, BUT REMOVE FROM THE FRIDGE FOR ABOUT 30 MINUTES BEFORE EATING.

MERINGUE
LOLLIES

Colourful meringues make wonderful party treats. The lollipop sticks transform these sweets into fun snacks that are sure to delight all ages. They can be wrapped up for wedding favours, arranged in jars for birthday parties or even used as cake decorations (see Electro-pop Drip Cake, page 134).

A B C D

Makes 16–20 lollies

Prep time, 30 minutes

Bake time, 1 hour to 1 hour 20 minutes

Ingredients

4 medium egg whites,
at room temperature

200g (7oz) white caster (superfine) sugar

Food colouring gel of your choice

Vanilla extract

100g (3½oz) white chocolate

Variety of edible flowers, I've used violas, bellis daisies, tiny tagetes, cornflower petals and calendulas

Equipment

Lollipop sticks

Piping bags

Large open star nozzle, I used a Wilton 1M nozzle

1 tsp vanilla extract, I used the Nielsen-Massey one

Small paintbrush

Method

1. Whisk the egg whites with an electric whisk until they form stiff peaks.

2. Slowly add the caster sugar, one spoonful at a time, beating well between each addition until the mixture is glossy and the sugar has been completely incorporated. Whisk in the vanilla.

3. Place the star nozzle into the piping bag and turn the bag inside out. To create pretty coloured streaks on the meringue, paint strips of food colouring onto the piping bag with a small, clean paintbrush (A and B).

WHEN ADDING COLOUR TO THE PIPING BAG, PAINTING 2–3 STRIPES IS PREFERABLE. YOU CAN USE MULTIPLE PIPING BAGS IF YOU WANT A RANGE OF DIFFERENT COLOURS.

4. Turn your piping bag the right way out and carefully fill with the meringue mixture (C and D).

>>>

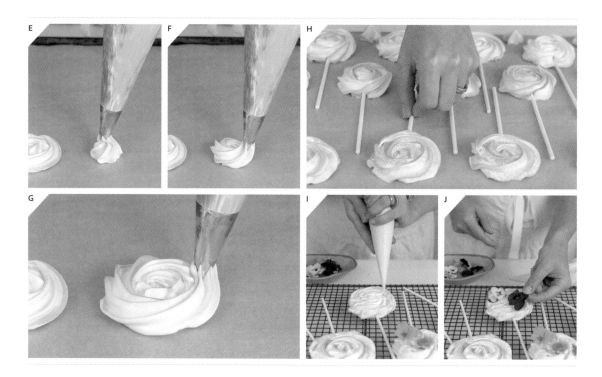

5. Holding the piping bag vertically over a lined baking tray, begin piping in the centre and work outwards to create a spiral (E and F). Stop squeezing the bag after a couple of rounds and pull the bag away from the tray (G). Repeat to cover the tray with piped meringue circles.

6. Push a lollipop stick into the bottom half of each circle (H).

7. Bake at 120°C (250°F) for 20 minutes and then turn the oven down to 100°C (210°F). Bake for a further 40–60 minutes until the meringues have completely dried out. Turn off the oven and leave to cool in the oven until you are ready to decorate.

8. Melt the white chocolate, either in a bain-marie or in a microwave on low heat, stirring every 30 seconds.

9. Place the melted chocolate in a piping bag and drizzle over each lolly (I). Decorate with edible flowers (J).

IF YOU DECIDE TO DECORATE THE MERINGUES WITH FRESH FLOWERS, THEY WILL NEED TO BE EATEN ON THE SAME DAY. HOWEVER, THE MERINGUE LOLLIES CAN BE BAKED IN ADVANCE, STORED FOR UP TO FIVE DAYS (IF KEPT WELL WRAPPED) AND DECORATED WHEN NEEDED. ALTERNATIVELY, CRYSTALLISED OR DRIED FLOWERS CAN BE USED, WHICH WILL NOT DETERIORATE AS THEY ARE PRESERVED.

SUGAR
LOLLIES

Choosing your assortment of edible flowers is the hardest part of making these adorable sugar lollies. These little treats are so easy to make, and they are perfect for capturing the flowers in all of their beauty. Once the flowers are suspended in the sugar, they are perfectly preserved and will not deteriorate.

A

B

C

D

Makes 8 lollies

Prep time, 20-30 minutes

Bake time, 20-30 minutes

Cooling time, approx 2-3 hours

Ingredients

Approximately 70 Glacier Mints (or clear boiled sweets)

Variety of edible flowers (rose petals, violas, fuchsias and bellis daisies work best)

Edible gold leaf (optional)

Equipment

Silicone lollipop mould, I used one from Silikomart

Lollipop sticks

Method

1. Place a layer of boiled sweets into the bottom of each lollipop mould, and then add lolly sticks in the openings of the mould.

> IF YOU DON'T HAVE A LOLLIPOP MOULD, YOU CAN USE A LINED BAKING TRAY TO CREATE ROUGHLY SHAPED, FLATTER SUGAR LOLLIES.

2. Place a selection of edible flowers and gold leaf, if using, into the moulds on top of the boiled sweets (A and B).

3. Carefully add another layer of boiled sweets on top of the flowers (C and D).

4. Bake at 150°C (300°F) for 20-30 minutes until the boiled sweets are fully melted.

5. As soon as the lollies come out of the oven, push the lollipop stick further into the base of each one. Leave to cool for 2-3 hours before removing from the mould.

> IF YOU LEAVE THESE LOLLIES UNWRAPPED THEY WILL START TO DISSOLVE DUE TO MOISTURE IN THE ATMOSPHERE. THEREFORE IF THEY ARE TO BE GIVEN AS GIFTS, WRAP THEM IN CELLOPHANE BAGS AND TIE TIGHTLY WITH TWINE OR RIBBON. THEY WILL KEEP FOR AT LEAST A WEEK.

DRIED FLOWERS CHOCOLATE BARK

I love making chocolate bark, it's so pretty and simple to create and makes the perfect treat. It's also lovely to use as a cake decoration. Using dried edible flowers gives you the lovely 'funfetti' effect without having to use tons of sweets and artificial colourings.

Makes 33 x 23cm (13 x 9in) of bark

Prep time, 20 minutes

Cooling time, 1–2 hours, depending on temperature of surroundings

Ingredients

500g (1lb 2oz) good-quality white chocolate

Dried flowers of your choice, I used a mix of whole and crumbled dried flowers including bellis daisies, amaranth, fire feathers, cornflower, calendula petals and some greenery

Equipment

Baking tray lined with greaseproof parchment paper, 33 x 23cm (13 x 9in)

Bain-marie, or microwave-safe bowl

Method

1. Melt the white chocolate gently either in a bain-marie or with a microwave on low-medium heat for 30 second blasts, stirring until just melted.

2. Pour the melted chocolate into the baking tray (A) and gently tap the tray on your work surface to settle the chocolate flat and get rid of any bubbles.

3. Decorate with your dried flowers, leaving some whole and crumbling some for finer details (B).

4. Allow to cool completely (C) then snap or cut up and serve, wrap or use for cake decorations (see Electro-pop Drip Cake, page 134).

CUPCAKE WREATH

This gorgeous wreath is so simple to make, the edible flowers do all the work for you to create a stunning centre piece. You can make these in any size you wish by building up rings of cupcakes, from mini to large. To construct this arrangement, unless you are using a huge plate, it is best to place the cakes on site where you wish to display them, and pipe the frosting on to connect them up then top with flowers.

Makes 20–24 standard cupcakes

Prep time, 1 hour

Bake time, 12–15 minutes

Ingredients

1.2kg (2lb 10½oz) vanilla sponge batter (see Very Vanilla Sponge Recipe, page 22)

1.5kg (3lb 5oz) vanilla buttercream (see Vanilla Buttercream recipe, page 24)

A selection of fresh edible flowers and leaves of your choice. I have used sweet cicely, zinnias, white cornflowers, pineapple sage, dahlias, roses, tagetes, alyssum and flowering mint

Equipment

Cupcake tins and cases in your choice of size. I used, 7.5cm (3in), 6cm (2⅜in) and 5cm (2in) diameter cases

Plastic piping bag with a large round 1cm (½in) nozzle, or cut a 1cm (½in) hole in the tip of a piping bag

Method

1. Preheat the oven to 180°C (350°F).

2. Follow the instructions in the Very Vanilla Sponge Recipe on page 22 to make the cupcake batter. Scrape the mixture into your cupcake cases or lined cupcake tins as required.

3. Bake for around 12–15 minutes, checking every few minutes. The cakes should be a light golden brown, springy to the touch. A sharp knife or metal skewer should come out clean and free of mixture.

»»

4. Leave to cool for a couple of minutes in the tins then turn the cupcakes out onto a cooling rack.

ONCE THE CUPCAKES ARE ICED THEY WILL LAST WELL FOR TWO TO THREE DAYS. IF FROZEN, THEY'LL KEEP FOR A MONTH. TO FREEZE, I USE A CORRUGATED CUPCAKE BOX WITH LITTLE INSERTS TO KEEP THEM IN SHAPE, THEN WRAP CLING FILM AROUND THE BOX. ALLOW THE CUPCAKES TO COME TO ROOM TEMPERATURE FOR 3-4 HOURS BEFORE USING. HOWEVER, THE FLOWERS WILL NOT KEEP IN THE FREEZER, YOU MUST USE THEM FRESH AND NOTE THAT THEY WILL START TO WILT AFTER A DAY OR TWO.

5. Arrange the cooled cupcakes in an eye-pleasing ring as the base of your wreath (A).

6. Make the buttercream following the Vanilla Buttercream recipe on page 24, then fill the piping bag. Pipe buttercream onto each cupcake in a circular motion (B), starting from the outside edge and spiralling towards the centre until the surface is completely covered.

7. Continue until all the cupcakes are covered in buttercream. This will begin to join them together where the buttercream overlaps a little from one cupcake to its neighbour (C).

8. While the buttercream is still fresh, begin to add the foliage and flowers starting with a few leaves. Build up the decoration by adding flowers, starting with the larger ones, then adding the smaller varieties (D).

9. Fill any gaps with small flowers until you are happy with the complete arrangement (E).

YOU CAN TAKE A FEW PIPING BAGS READY LOADED WITH YOU TO YOUR CHOSEN VENUE IF YOU ARE MAKING A VERY LARGE WREATH. IN MY DESIGN I'VE USED A MIX OF AROUND 35 CUPCAKES IN MEDIUM, SMALL AND MINI SIZES TO CREATE A REALLY LOVELY LARGE WREATH.

GANACHE TRIO

This delicious trio of chocolatey treats are all based on the same ganache recipe, with some additions to create decadent tartlets, truffles and a luscious chocolate ganache frosting for cupcakes. All accessorised, of course, with gorgeous edible flowers in fresh, dried and crystallised form.

GANACHE CUPCAKES

These cupcakes are very special and worthy of the best party or gathering... perfect for a wedding, in fact. Those fabulous crystallised dahlias – so special!

Makes 12–16 large cupcakes

Prep time, 45 minutes

Bake time, 15–20 minutes

Ingredients

175g (6oz) dark (bittersweet) chocolate chips (70% cocoa solids)

200g (7oz) light muscovado sugar

175g (6oz) soft, salted butter, plus extra for greasing

3 medium eggs and 2 egg yolks

100g (3½oz) soured (sour) cream

1 tsp vanilla extract

150g (5½oz) self-raising (-rising) flour

2 tbsp cocoa powder (unsweetened cocoa)

500g (1lb 2oz) vanilla buttercream (see Vanilla Buttercream recipe, page 24)

Crystallised flowers of your choice, I've used dahlias

CHOCOLATE GANACHE

300g (10½oz) dark (bittersweet) chocolate, finely chopped or in chocolate chips

190ml (6¾fl oz) double (heavy) cream

FOR THE CUPCAKES YOU'LL JUST NEED HALF THIS QUANTITY FOR STIRRING ONTO THE BUTTERCREAM. THE REST CAN BE FROZEN FOR UP TO ONE MONTH OR KEPT IN THE FRIDGE FOR A WEEK.

Equipment

Bain-marie or heat-proof or microwave-proof bowl

Muffin tray

Cupcake cases

Plastic piping bag, with a large open star nozzle, I used a Wilton 1M

>>>

Method

1. Preheat the oven to 180ºC (350ºF).

2. Place the chocolate, sugar and butter in a microwave-proof bowl. Put in the microwave and heat on a medium setting for 1 minute intervals, stirring at each interval, until everything is melted together. Alternatively, melt in a bain-marie or heat-proof bowl over a pan of simmering water. Do not allow the bowl to touch the water. Allow to cool slightly.

3. Whisk the eggs, soured cream and vanilla extract together. Mix together the flour and cocoa powder.

4. Add the egg mixture to the melted chocolate mix and stir well, then fold in the flour and cocoa.

5. Spoon the batter into cupcake cases in the muffin tray to just over half full.

6. Bake for 15–20 minutes until just firm. A testing knife or skewer should come out slightly paste-y (but not wet) when it's cooked (not clean, as you'd expect from a vanilla sponge). Leave to cool in the muffin tray.

7. To make the ganache, roughly chop the chocolate and place in a bowl.

8. Heat the cream until just boiling and then pour over the chocolate (A). Mix until the chocolate has fully melted and leave to cool to room temperature (B).

9. Divide the ganache in half and save the excess. Stir the ganache into the buttercream with a spoon or in a mixer on slow until creamy and chocolatey and load into a plastic piping bag with a large open star nozzle.

10. Pipe a swirl of frosting onto each cupcake (C). Hold the bag vertically so you are piping directly from above. Begin piping a thick circle of frosting around the outside edge of the case, to cover the edge, then in one continuous motion, continue piping the swirl in a circle inwards and upwards so you have a lovely whipped chocolate ganache frosting.

11. Finish your cupcakes with a whole crystallised dahlia (see Crystallising Edible Flowers, page 17) (D).

GANACHE TARTLETS

Complement the special cupcakes with these decadent tartlets - a crisp hazelnut case brimming with glorious ganache and topped with flowers.

A

B

C

Makes 6-8 tartlets

Prep time, 45 minutes

Bake time, 20-30 minutes

Chill time approx 20-30 minutes

Ingredients

120g (4¼oz) cold diced slightly salted butter

250g (9oz) plain (all-purpose) flour plus a little extra for rolling

80g (3oz) finely chopped toasted hazelnuts

2-4 tbsp cold water

Chocolate ganache filling (see ingredients for chocolate ganache in Ganache Cupcakes, page 54), plus 40ml (1½fl oz) honey

Fresh violas

Edible gold leaf (optional)

Equipment

Individual tart cases, I used six 10cm (4in) diameter ones

Food processor or bowl and fingertips

Rolling pin

Baking parchment

Baking beans or dry rice/pasta for blind baking

Saucepan

Mixing bowl

Sharp knife

Method

1. In a food processor blitz together the butter and flour until they resemble breadcrumbs. You can also do this in a bowl and rub the flour and butter with the tips of your fingers.

2. Add the hazelnuts and mix, and then slowly add the water until the dough forms.

3. Sprinkle the surface with flour and roll out the pastry to 2-3mm (⅟₁₆-⅛in) thick.

4. Cut it into six pieces and gently press the pastry into the tart cases (A). Press a rolling pin over the top of the case to neatly trim off the excess pastry. If it breaks do not worry, just patch it up with pastry and press it into the tin with your fingers.

5. Line the tarts with parchment and fill with baking beans (B).

6. Bake for 10-15 minutes at 190°C (375°F) then remove the tarts from the oven and take out the baking beans. Then continue to bake for a further 10-15 minutes until golden brown.

7. Make the ganache following steps 7 and 8 in the Ganache Cupcakes instructions, but stir in the honey at the end and do not allow it cool too much, or it will start to set (C).

>>>

8. Pour the ganache into the tart cases (D) and chill for 20–30 minutes until the ganache is set.

9. Decorate with violas (E) and gold leaf (F) just before serving. Use a sharp knife to cut small pieces of the gold leaf and don't try to pick them up with your fingers, but use the tip of your knife to transfer them to the top of the tartlet.

YOU CAN MAKE THE PASTRY CASES IN ADVANCE AND STORE THEM IN AN AIRTIGHT CONTAINER OR BAG FOR THREE DAYS, THEN FILL THEM WITH THE GANACHE WHEN READY TO SERVE. THEY WILL ALSO KEEP FROZEN FOR UP TO A MONTH BEFORE OR AFTER BAKING. DRESS WITH FLOWERS (IF USING FRESH) WHEN READY TO SERVE.

GANACHE TRUFFLES

Perfect indulgent treats that get better with the addition of dried flowers – try them and you'll see what I mean.

Makes 15–20, depending on size

Prep time, 30 minutes

Chill time, approx 1 hour

Ingredients

Chocolate ganache centres (see ingredients for chocolate ganache in Ganache Cupcakes, page 54, plus 40ml (1½fl oz) honey, or shot of your favourite tipple (optional)

200g (7oz) milk chocolate

Dried flowers of your choice, I've used a mix of cornflowers, mixed colour dianthus, amaranth and calendula along with their greenery

Equipment

Baking tray lined with parchment paper

Bowls

Bain-marie, or a microwave-proof bowl

Cocktail sticks (toothpicks) or wooden skewers

Method

1. To make the ganache, follow steps 7 and 8 in Ganache Cupcakes, page 56, stirring in the honey/alcohol at the end.

2. Place the ganache in the fridge to chill until set (about 30 minutes).

3. Make the truffle balls by scooping a large walnut-sized amount of ganache into your palms. Roll to create little round balls (A), place them on a baking tray and leave to chill again for 30 minutes while you prepare the chocolate coating.

4. Melt the chocolate gently over a bain-marie or in a microwave on low-medium heat for 30 second blasts until just melted. Allow to cool slightly before coating the truffle balls.

5. To coat, spear each ball on a wooden skewer or cocktail stick (B), dunk in the cooled chocolate (C) and tap gently on the side of the bowl to let any excess chocolate drip away.

6. Place the truffle on a clean tray lined with baking parchment (you can use an extra cocktail stick if you need to push it off the dipping stick) (D).

7. Sprinkle the truffles with a pretty mix of dried edible flowers and leave to set (E).

STORE IN THE FRIDGE FOR UP TO ONE WEEK, BUT REMOVE FOR AN HOUR OR TWO BEFORE SERVING.

CHOUXNUTS

I love these light and airy pastries. They're perfect for a special afternoon tea, or as part of a dessert table for a big occasion. Similar to an éclair, but piped in a circle, they look like doughnuts. So cute! I've used oregano flowers to decorate but you could use any fresh flowers you fancy.

60

Makes 15–20 chouxnuts, depending on size

Prep time, 1 hour

Bake time, 25–35 minutes

Ingredients

CRÈME PÂTISSIÈRE

4 egg yolks

60g (2¼oz) sugar

25g (1oz) plain (all-purpose) flour

2 tsp cornflour (cornstarch)

280ml (10fl oz) milk

CHOUX PASTRY

225ml (8fl oz) water

110g (3¾oz) butter

130g (4¾oz) plain (all-purpose) flour

225g (8oz) free-range egg

Pinch of salt

2 tbsp caster (superfine) sugar

CHANTILLY CREAM, BASE FOR CRÈME DIPLOMAT

300ml (10½fl oz) double (heavy) cream

2 tbsp icing (confectioner's) sugar

2 tsp vanilla bean paste

FONDANT TOPPING

300g (10½oz) fondant icing (frosting) sugar

Water and food colouring of your choice, I used a cream colour

Edible flowers of your choice, I've used oregano flowers, pink butterfly sorrel and alyssum

Equipment

Baking tray(s)

Baking parchment

Circle for drawing round, I used a few cookie cutters

Large plastic piping bag with medium to large round nozzle

Method

1. Preheat the oven to 190°C (375°F) and line two baking trays with baking parchment.

2. In a pan heat the water, sugar, salt and butter until completely melted.

3. Add the flour and beat well on the heat for 4–5 minutes until the dough comes away from the pan edges easily.

4. Transfer the dough into a bowl and leave it to cool for 2–3 minutes.

5. Slowly add the egg bit-by-bit, beating well until the choux is the right consistency. It should be stiff, but it should easily drop off a spoon.

6. Put the choux paste into a piping bag with a medium to large round nozzle.

7. Draw around a circular cutter (size of your choice) onto the baking parchment (A), flip the paper over and then pipe the circles of choux following the guide circles (B).

⋙

8. Place the trays into the oven; spray some water onto the base of the oven before shutting the door (this creates a steamy environment in the oven which helps the pastry to rise).

9. Bake for 25-35 minutes. Do not open the door of the oven until at least 25 minutes into baking otherwise the chouxnuts will collapse.

10. Transfer the chouxnuts to a wire rack to cool. Make a small hole in the base of each chouxnut with a small knife or skewer to let the steam out (C) and leave upside down on the wire rack to cool completely.

11. To make the crème pâtissière, first beat the egg yolks and sugar with the vanilla and the flours until pale and thickened.

12. Heat the milk in a pan until just boiling, whisk the milk into the egg mix and then pour it back into the pan.

13. Heat the mixture stirring continuously until it is thick and boiling.

14. Take it off the heat and pour it onto a tray and cover with cling film making sure the cling film is touching the crème pâtissière to stop a skin forming.

15. Once the crème pâtissière has cooled, in a bowl whisk 300ml (10½fl oz) of double cream with the icing sugar and vanilla to soft peak stage (this is a Chantilly cream). Gently mix the crème pâtissière into the Chantilly cream until smooth, light and fluffy to make your Crème Diplomat filling.

IF YOU WANT TO DO A QUICKER VERSION OF THESE, YOU CAN SIMPLY FILL THE CHOUXNUTS WITH CHANTILLY CREAM. THEY WILL BE LOVELY AND FRESH, BUT THE CRÈME DIPLOMAT IS A DELICIOUS CUSTARDY FILLING THAT IS VERY SPECIAL INDEED.

16. Poke a hole into the base of your chouxnuts with a small knife and then pipe in the cream until you can feel that the chouxnuts are full (D). You can feel them getting heavy in your hand.

17. Leave the chouxnuts to one side.

18. To make the fondant, weigh 300g (10½oz) fondant icing sugar and slowly add water 1 tsp at a time until you have a thick icing consistency. I added a little cream colouring to the fondant at this stage, but you could leave it white.

19. Using a piping bag, pipe a ring of icing onto the chouxnuts (E and F) and tap them on the surface to help the icing settle (G). Then decorate with edible flowers of your choice (H and I).

THESE ARE BEST EATEN FRESH BUT WILL KEEP IN THE FRIDGE FOR TWO DAYS, BUT THE PASTRY WILL LOSE ITS CRISPNESS.

FLORAL KRISPIE CAKE TOPPER

Using Rice Krispies is one of my favourite ways to make three-dimensional structures as they are really lightweight and, with marshmallows added, hold their shape well (plus this mix is pretty tasty and reminds me of being a child!). You can make a template and cut any shape you like.

Makes any shape 23 x 33cm (9 x 13in)

Prep time, 1 hour

Chill time, approx 1 hour

Ingredients

45g (2oz) butter

300g (10½oz) miniature marshmallows

150g (5½oz) Rice Krispies cereal

1 tsp vanilla bean paste or extract

100g (3½oz) white chocolate

Fresh edible flowers of your choice, I've used pansies, violas, snapdragons, fire feathers, calendulas, carnations and small yellow roses

YOU CAN USE STANDARD-SIZE LARGE MARSHMALLOWS, BUT CUT THEM INTO SMALLER CHUNKS WITH SCISSORS TO MAKE IT EASIER TO MELT THEM.

Equipment

Baking tray lined with oiled baking parchment, 23 x 33 x 3cm (9 x 13 x 1¼in)

Card for template

Sharp knife

Lolly sticks

Method

1. In large saucepan melt the butter over a low heat. Add the marshmallows and vanilla, stirring until completely melted. Then remove the mixture from the heat.

2. Tip in the cereal and stir until well coated. Alternatively, you can make this recipe in a large bowl by heating the butter and marshmallows in a microwave on high for a minute at a time, stirring in between, for 2–3 minutes. Then stir in the vanilla, tip in the Krispies and stir.

3. Using a buttered spatula or baking paper, evenly press the warm mixture into the parchment lined tray. Place in the fridge for an hour or so until completely set.

4. To create the letters or numbers, make a card template (see Templates, page 140, for the one I have used here) and with a sharp knife, carefully cut around it to reveal your Krispie treat shape (A). If using as a cake topper, push in a lolly stick or two about half way into the shape to give it stability and help to fix it onto your cake (B).

5. To stick on the flowers, brush the Rice Krispie shape with melted white chocolate (C) and press the flowers on and around the shape to fit and flow with the curves (D). The fire feathers are good for bending around curves and of course smaller flowers will help to go around smaller details or fill any gaps.

JUST
DESSERTS

SPRING FLOWERS
BUNDT CAKE

I am a huge fan of Bundt cakes, they are so pretty and yet homely. I've acquired a
large collection of Bundt tins over the years, in so many shapes and sizes (I'm a big
Nordicware fan too!). The tins do all the work for you by producing a gorgeous sculptural
sponge - just add some orange blossom fondant and crystallised primroses!

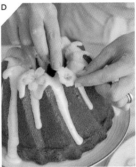

Serves 10–12

Prep time, 30 minutes

Bake time, 35–45 minutes

Ingredients

SPONGE

250g (9oz) butter

200g (7oz) plain (all-purpose) flour

50g (1¾oz) ground almonds

1 tsp baking powder

225g (8oz) golden caster (superfine)
sugar

1 tsp vanilla extract

2 tsp orange blossom water, I used
the Nielsen-Massey one

Zest of 1 orange

4 medium free-range eggs

FONDANT

200g (7oz) fondant icing
(confectioner's) sugar

1 tsp orange blossom water

Zest of 1 orange

2–3 tsp water to loosen to desired
consistency

Crystallised flowers, I've used
primroses

Equipment

Stand mixer, hand whisk or bowl and
wooden spoon

Bundt tin, I've used a Nordicware
Kugelhopf one – I love the tallness
of it!

Pastry brush

Piping bag

Method

1. Preheat the oven to 170°C (335°F)
and prepare your Bundt tin by brushing
the inside with melted butter, dusting
with flour and shaking out the excess
(or use cake release spray) (A).

2. Cream the butter, sugar, zest and
flavourings together in a stand mixer
or by hand until very pale and fluffy.

3. Beat in the eggs gently one by one
until fully incorporated.

4. In a separate bowl lightly mix the
almonds, flour and baking powder to
distribute all evenly then gently mix
into the wet ingredients.

5. Pour into the tin, level off and bake
for approximately 35–45 minutes, until
cooked through. Use a cake tester in
the centre to check. Turn the cake out
and leave it to cool on a rack.

6. Meanwhile mix your fondant sugar,
zest, orange blossom and water to a
dripping (but not runny) consistency (B).

7. Pipe all over your cake so the
fondant flows into the crevices and
over the pattern of your Bundt (C).
Decorate with flowers (D).

GIN AND TONIC
CAKE TAILS

I love these playful desserts - my take on a layered style jar cake, or a trifle and cocktail combo. They are perfect for parties and with the violas suspended in the jelly, so beautiful! These are quite labour intensive, but to cut out a stage you can use a store bought curd and add some colouring.

Serves 6 (depending on glass size)

Prep time, 1 hour

Bake time, 20–25 minutes

Chill time, approx 1 hour

Setting time, 4 hours

Ingredients

SPONGE

150g (5½oz) butter

150g (5½oz) caster (superfine) sugar

3 medium free-range eggs

Zest of 1 large grapefruit

150g (5½oz) self-raising (-rising) flour

½ tsp baking powder

GRAPEFRUIT CURD

2 large free-range eggs plus one yolk

2 tsp cornflour (cornstarch)

Juice and zest of 1 grapefruit

75g (2¾oz) unsalted butter

Pink food colouring

JELLY

125ml (4½fl oz) tonic

65g (2⅜oz) caster (superfine) sugar

60ml (2¼fl oz) gin

65ml (2⅜fl oz) water

4 leaves of gelatine

MASCARPONE LAYER

250g (9oz) mascarpone

200g (7oz) grapefruit curd

50ml (1¾fl oz) gin

Fresh and crystallised violas

Equipment

Stand mixer, electric whisk or bowl and wooden spoon

6 glasses for serving, I used 250ml (9fl oz) capacity glasses

Piping bags

18cm (7in) square cake tin, lined with baking parchment

Round cutter, suitable size for your serving glasses

Cling film (plastic wrap)

Method

1. Make the curd first, you can do this a day or two in advance if you wish. Mix the cornflour with the eggs and colouring and set aside.

2. Heat the sugar, zest and juice until the sugar is dissolved and the mix is hot but not boiling. In a separate pan, off the heat, add the egg mix and then pour over the hot sugar mix whisking well the whole time.

3. Return to the heat, stirring constantly and heat on low as the sauce thickens, this can take up to 10 minutes. Remove from the heat.

4. Once cool, chill in the fridge until needed, covered to prevent a skin forming - make sure the cling film is touching the surface of the curd.

>>>

5. Next make the sponge: in either a stand mixer, electric whisk or by hand, cream the butter, sugar, grapefruit zest and food colouring together until pale and fluffy.

6. Add the eggs gradually until incorporated then fold in the flour.

7. Spread into the tin, level off and bake for 20–25 minutes at 180°C (350°F), until the edges shrink away from the tin and the sponge is cooked through. Leave to cool.

8. Next make the gin and tonic jelly: soak the gelatine in a bowl, then heat the water, juice and sugar in a pan.

9. Once the sugar mix is hot add the gelatine (squeeze out the excess water first) to the pan and mix well.

10. Add the gin and tonic and pour into a jug.

11. Now you can assemble your desserts: pour the first of four shallow layers of gin and tonic jelly into each glass and add an edible flower, pushing it below the surface of the jelly for the first layer (A). As it is only a shallow layer it won't take long to set in the fridge. Repeat with three further layers to build up a pretty base of suspended flowers in the bottom of each glass.

12. Once the jelly is set, make the mascarpone layer. Beat the mascarpone until soft, add 200g (7oz) of curd to this and two shots of gin, and beat well until creamy. Place into a large plastic piping bag and snip the tip of the bag.

13. Pipe a thin layer of mascarpone filling over the jelly (B).

14. Cut a sponge disc out to fit into the glass (C), leaving a little room around the edge. Push the sponge disc into the glass (D) and pipe extra mascarpone filing around the sponge and over the top to cover (E).

15. Lastly add a layer of curd to finish (F). Top each glass with a little cling film and chill for an hour to set. Keep in the fridge, then remove the cling film and top with a crystallised viola when ready to serve (G).

THESE WILL LAST FOR TWO DAYS. YOU CAN COVER THE GLASSES WITH CLING FILM ONCE ASSEMBLED, AND THEN WHEN YOU ARE READY TO SERVE, BRING OUT FROM THE FRIDGE FOR AN HOUR AND TOP OFF WITH FLOWERS.

PISTACHIO, MINT AND YOGHURT CAKE

This fresh and light recipe is covered in lightly sweetened yoghurt. When arranged with fruit and flowers to top off the delicious sponge it is a perfect combination, and very simple to decorate.

A  B  C  D

Serves 10–12

Prep time, 50 minutes

Bake time, 40–50 minutes

Chill time, minimum 1 hour

Ingredients

SYRUP

100ml (3½fl oz) water

100g (3½oz) caster (superfine) sugar

50g (1¾oz) honey

Handful of chopped mint

CAKE

240g (8½oz) self-raising (-rising) flour

Pinch of salt

300g (10½oz) blitzed pistachios

200g (7oz) butter

350g (12oz) caster (superfine) sugar

50g (1¾oz) honey

2 tbsp fresh mint

8 eggs

YOGHURT TOPPING

250g (9oz) full-fat Greek yoghurt

2 tbsp icing (confectioner's) sugar

2 tbsp honey

Fresh fruits, I've used green, gold and baby kiwi slices, and slices of orange, strawberries and blueberries

Flowering mint leaves and edible flowers to decorate, I've used mixed colour zinnias and flowering mint

Equipment

Stand mixer, electric whisk or bowl and wooden spoon

Cake leveller or sharp knife

Palette knife

23cm (9in) round cake tin, lined with baking parchment

Method

1. Cream the butter and sugar until light and fluffy, then add the eggs one at a time until combined.

2. Add the mint and honey, and fold in the flour, pistachios and salt.

3. Bake at 160°C (325°F) for 40–50 minutes until cooked through.

4. Make the yoghurt topping in a bowl. Add the honey and sugar to the yoghurt and stir through (A).

5. Trim off the hump from the top of the cake (B and C).

6. Spoon the yoghurt topping onto the cake and using a palette knife, level and make it smooth.

7. Go around the edge of the cake with the palette knife to make it neat and round and so that the topping sits around the edge of the sponge (D).

> YOU CAN ADD THE TOPPING TO THE CAKE, IN ADVANCE, AND KEEP IN THE FRIDGE FOR A FEW HOURS BEFORE DRESSING IT WITH FRUIT AND FLOWERS.

8. Dress with fruit and fresh flowers, trimming the fruit and choosing various sizes of flowers so they fit neatly together and around the top edge of the cake. Chill for at least an hour before serving.

JELLY AND CREAM SPONGE CAKE

A very special cake indeed – the jelly layer, sponge and cream filling create an amazing taste combination and the prosecco and elderflower jelly is to die for! This dessert is very light, a wonderful finish for any feast, and although it's fairly labour intensive I promise you will love it, and your guests will be extremely impressed.

A

Serves 8-10

Prep time, 1 hour

Bake time, 15 minutes

Chill time, 4 hours or overnight

Ingredients

GENOESE SPONGE

320g (11⅜oz) eggs

180g (6⅛oz) caster (superfine) sugar

180g (6⅛oz) plain (all-purpose) flour

2 tsp vanilla bean paste

30g (1oz) melted butter

Generous pinch of salt

CREAM FILLING

300ml (10½fl oz) double (heavy) cream

100g (3½oz) fresh raspberries

50g (1¾oz) caster (superfine) sugar, plus 2 tbsp

1 tsp vanilla extract

1 gelatine leaf

3 tbsp boiling water

JELLY

750ml (25½fl oz, 1 standard bottle) prosecco

150ml (5fl oz) elderflower cordial

7 leaves of gelatine

1 tbsp caster (superfine) sugar

Edible flowers of your choice, I've used pansies, violas, dianthus petals and flowering mint leaves

Equipment

Electric hand whisk

23cm (9in) round or square cake tin

Cling film (plastic wrap)

20cm (8in) mousse ring, 7.5cm (3in) depth, or round spring form tin

10cm (4in) deep acetate strip long enough to line the inside of the ring/tin

Large mixing bowl

Cake leveller or sharp knife

Cake lifter (optional)

Method

1. Fix the size of the acetate ring by slotting it inside your mousse ring or spring form tin (A). Once you are sure the size of the ring matches the tin, tape the ends together. Next, grease and line a 23cm (9in) cake tin, and preheat the oven to 190°C (375°F).

>>>

2. Whisk the eggs, sugar, salt and vanilla for 6–8 minutes until four times the volume and very pale, light and fluffy.

3. Very gently fold in the flour and then pour the mixture carefully into the lined tin. Tip the tin gently to make it level.

4. Bake for 10–15 minutes until light and springy, and cake tester or skewer comes out clean. Remove from the tin and leave to cool.

5. Next make the jelly: soak the gelatine leaves in cold water, then place the cordial, sugar and 150ml (5fl oz) of prosecco in a saucepan and bring to the boil.

6. Squeeze the gelatine to remove the excess water then place it in the hot mixture and stir until dissolved.

7. Add the rest of the prosecco carefully, avoiding too much fizzing, and mix gently. Leave to cool for 10–15 minutes.

8. To create the jelly layer, line a baking tray that is a little larger than 20cm (8in) carefully with cling film and place on it a 20cm (8in) spring form tin without its base or a mousse ring, and then bring the cling film up around the outside edge of the ring.

9. Next add your suspended flowers in the jelly. Begin by pouring one quarter of the jelly mixture into the ring (B) and place flowers around the jelly making sure you place a few facing outwards so it looks really pretty (C).

10. Set this in the fridge for approximately 30–40 minutes until completely set.

11. Repeat the process twice more adding flowers so they stay suspended at different levels.

12. Finish the ring by adding a final layer of plain jelly, without flowers. Leave it to set for a few hours until you are ready to assemble your creation.

G

H

I

J

K

13. Next, make the cream filling: soak the gelatine in cold water for a few minutes. Squeeze out the excess water, then gently melt the gelatine by stirring in a small pan with 3 tbsp of boiling water and 2 tbsp of caster sugar. Allow this syrup to cool.

14. Whisk the cream, vanilla and sugar to soft peaks.

15. Gently fold in the raspberries and then add the gelatine syrup, folding it through.

16. Using a cake leveller or long sharp bread knife, carefully slice the sponge in half through the middle to make two layers.

17. Cut around your mousse ring (or spring form tin) to give you two rounds of sponge (D).

18. Place the ring on your chosen cake stand or plate and line with an additional length of acetate strip to support your structure and aid removal.

19. Carefully lift a layer of sponge (a cake lifter will help as the sponge is so delicate) and place the base layer of cake in the ring (E), pushing it down with your hands.

20. Spoon in the cream filling (F) and smooth over to level, then top with the second sponge and push that down firmly to bond and level everything well. Chill the filled cake for 30 minutes.

21. Remove the ring and acetate (G and H), and carefully tip the jelly onto a cling-film-lined cake leveller or flat cake board/plate to aid moving the delicate jelly (I), flip over and remove the cling film from under the jelly (J).

22. Now, confidently and quickly using the lifter or board, flip the jelly centrally on to your sponges (K), you can carefully shift the jelly slightly to fit if need be but try to get as much on as centrally as possible.

23. If desired dress your stand with additional flowers, step back, admire and serve!

ROSE AND LYCHEE CAKE

I really struggle to choose my favourite cake from this book... but I think this may be it. It tastes like rosy heaven and it is stunning. To crystallise all those petals will take a couple of hours, but I think it's worth the effort! I've created an ombre effect from cream to pink, but you could tailor this to suit any colour scheme.

Serves 10–12

Prep time, 2 hours

Bake time, 30-35 minutes

Chill time, 30 minutes to 1 hour

Ingredients

1 can (454g/1lb) lychee in syrup

240g (8½oz) self-raising (-rising) flour, sifted

2 tsp baking powder

½ tsp salt

240g (8½oz) unsalted butter, room temperature

180g (6⅛oz) golden caster (superfine) sugar

3 eggs

2 tsp vanilla extract

400g (14oz) vanilla buttercream (see Vanilla Buttercream recipe, page 24)

1 tsp rose water, I used the Nielsen-Massey one

Plenty of crystallised rose petals, if you wish to recreate an ombre effect choose at least three shades, I used about 250 petals on this cake

Equipment

2 round cake tins, 5 x 15cm (2 x 6in)

Palette knife

Method

1. Strain the lychees and set aside the syrup.

2. Cut the lychees into quarters and dry them between paper towels.

3. Cream the butter and sugar together until pale and fluffy.

4. Beat in the eggs one at a time, followed by the vanilla extract.

5. Sift the flour, baking powder and salt together and then fold them into the creamed butter mixture, pausing from time to time to add part of the 100ml (3½fl oz) reserved lychee syrup, until that is all incorporated too.

>>>

A   B   C   D

6. Fold half of the prepared lychees into the batter.

7. Portion the batter into two greased and lined 15cm (6in) round baking tins.

8. Then make a batch of buttercream (see Vanilla Buttercream, page 24), and add the rose water and the remaining lychees to it.

9. Layer the sponges with buttercream between them, then crumb coat the outside of the cake with buttercream using a palette knife (A) (see Crumb Coating, page 26).

10. Apply a thicker layer of buttercream for the crystallised rose petals to adhere to. This layer doesn't need to be completely smooth as it will be covered by the petals (B).

11. Starting on the top of the cake, apply the palest crystallised rose petals in a circle (C).

12. Continue to apply petals in circles of increasing size, gradually changing the petal colours as you get to the sides, until you reach the base with the darkest petals (D).

APPLE BLOSSOM
LOAF CAKE

This delicious teatime loaf cake is relatively quick and easy to make, so it's a great last-minute bake. The apple blossom flowers add a unique, elegant detail on top of the pretty pink apple icing. Apple blossom has a lovely delicate apple flavour, is a little sweet and has a nice soft bite. Pass the tea!

Serves 12-16

Prep time, 30 minutes

Bake time, 45-60 minutes

Chill time, 1 hour

Ingredients

100g (3½oz) salted butter

250g (9oz) self-raising (-rising) flour

125g (4½oz) muscovado sugar

3-4 tsp ground ginger

2 large cooking apples

4 eggs

1 tsp vanilla bean paste

100g (3½oz) fondant icing (confectioner's) sugar

1-2 tsp apple juice

Pink food colouring (optional)

Apple blossoms

Equipment

1kg (2lb) loaf tin, lined with baking parchment

Method

1. Rub the butter and flour together in a large bowl until you have a breadcrumb consistency.

2. Add the muscovado sugar and ground ginger, and mix well.

3. Peel the apples, cut into small chunks and stir into the dry mixture.

4. Gently beat the eggs and vanilla bean paste in a small bowl. Add to the dry ingredients and mix well.

5. Place the batter into a lined 1kg (2lb) loaf tin and bake at 170°C (335°F) for 45-60 minutes until cooked through, risen and golden on top. Leave to cool on a wire rack.

6. Mix the fondant icing sugar with apple juice until it reaches a runny consistency. Add a little pink food colouring if using. Drizzle the icing generously over the cake, allowing it to drip over the sides. Add a line of apple blossom flowers to decorate the top of the cake.

THE LOAF CAKE WILL KEEP FOR UP TO THREE DAYS IN AN AIRTIGHT CONTAINER, BUT IT IS BEST EATEN WHILE FRESH. THE APPLE BLOSSOM WILL START TO DETERIORATE AFTER A COUPLE OF DAYS.

ULTIMATE VEGAN CHOC CAKE

This recipe came about because of my daughter, Ruby. Since becoming vegan a couple of years ago she has really missed a good gooey chocolate fudge cake. We started experimenting and after several attempts, we think we nailed it with a cake that is delicious, whether you are vegan or not.

Serves 10–12

Prep time, 30 minutes

Cook time, 30 minutes

Chill time, approx 1 hour

Ingredients

VEGAN GANACHE FROSTING

250g (9oz) good-quality dark (bittersweet) chocolate chopped in small pieces (dairy free of course, I love Guittard)

100g (3½oz) dairy-free alternative cream of your choice

250g (9oz) non-dairy spread of your choice

600g (1lb 5oz) unrefined icing (confectioner's) sugar, Billington's do a good one

2 tsp vanilla bean paste

VEGAN CHOCOLATE FUDGE CAKE

350ml (12fl oz) soy or almond milk, or coconut milk if you love it a bit coconutty like I do

200g (7oz) coconut yoghurt

2 tsp apple cider vinegar

400g (14oz) light muscovado sugar

250ml (9fl oz) sunflower oil

2 tsp vanilla extract or vanilla bean paste

350g (12oz) self-raising (-rising) flour

130g (4¾oz) cocoa powder (unsweetened)

1 tsp baking powder

1 tsp bicarbonate of soda

½ tsp salt

Crystallised flowers of your choice, I've used violas, snapdragons, rose petals, cornflowers and fuchsias and crystallised them in a vegan-friendly way without egg white (see Vegan-friendly Crystallising, page 17)

Equipment

3 round cake tins, 18cm (7in) diameter

Stand mixer, electric whisk or bowl and wooden spoon

Cling film (plastic wrap)

Cake lifter or thin cake board

Palette knife

Method

1. Make the vegan ganache first by boiling the cream and pouring it over the chocolate. Cover the bowl with cling film and leave to sit for 2 minutes.

2. Remove the cling film and stir with a wooden spoon in the centre until you have a smooth creamy ganache. Set aside to cool.

>>>

3. Preheat the oven to 180°C (350°F). Grease three 18cm (7in) round tins and line the bases with baking parchment (or use two 20cm/8in tins instead).

4. Whisk together the almond/soy/coconut milk and vinegar in a large jug; the milk should curdle slightly.

5. Whisk in the sugar, oil and vanilla extract.

6. In a large bowl, mix together the flour, cocoa powder, baking powder, bicarbonate of soda and salt.

7. Gradually whisk the wet ingredients into the dry until smooth. Be careful not to over-mix. Divide the batter evenly between the tins and bake for about 30 minutes, until a skewer inserted into the centre comes out a little paste-y, but not wet/glistening. Slightly under baked makes for a fudgy cake!

YOU CAN MAKE THE FROSTING (SEE STEP 9) WHILE THE CAKES ARE BAKING.

8. Leave the cakes to cool in their tins for 30 minutes then carefully turn them out onto a wire rack to cool completely (they are soft and delicate so be gentle, it is helpful to use a cake lifter if you have one or a thin cake board to avoid cracking).

9. To make the frosting, beat the non-dairy spread, vanilla and icing sugar until pale, light and fluffy. Then add the cooled ganache and beat again until smooth and creamy.

IF YOU CAN'T GET HOLD OF UNREFINED ICING SUGAR FOR THE FROSTING, THE REGULAR SORT WORKS BUT IT DOESN'T HAVE THAT RICH CARAMEL TASTE.

10. To assemble the cake, place one of the layers on a serving plate or cake stand. Layer up and sandwich the layers with the frosting (A and B), then crumb coat all over the cake (see Crumb Coating, page 26) (C and D), and chill for 30 minutes to an hour.

11. Add a second covering of frosting – I like to cover the cake in luscious flicks of frosting (E), then top off with sugary crystallised flowers (F).

CELEBRATION
CAKES

FLOWERFETTI
INSIDE OUT CAKE

Decorating buttercream-covered sponges in an array of real edible flower petals is so simple to do, but super pretty! My lovely friend Bee from Bee's Bakery uses loads of edible flowers and inspired me to add 'flowerfetti' inside the sponge too. A feast for the eyes and the belly!

Serves 24–30

Prep time, 1 hour

Cook time, 20–25 minutes

Ingredients

Two-tier vanilla sponge cake with added lavender and petals (see below), with round tiers of 10cm (4in) and 18cm (7in) diameter

4–5 fresh sprigs of lavender and additional flower petals

1.1kg (2lb 7½oz) vanilla buttercream, see Vanilla Buttercream recipe, page 24

Tiny flowers and flower petals of your choice, I used tiny tagetes, lavender, violas, rose petals, calendula petals, fuchsias, cornflowers and greenery from these flowers

Equipment

Stand mixer, electric hand whisk or bowl and spoon

Baking parchment

Palette knife

Mixing bowls

Round cake tins, 10cm (4in) and 18cm (7in) diameter, or size of your choice (see below)

Cake board

Method

1. Make 1.1kg (2lb 7½oz) of vanilla cake batter (see Very Vanilla Sponge Recipe, page 22), then stir through the lavender and petals (A).

2. Line the base and sides of your cake tin or tins, and bake for 20–25 minutes at 180°C (350°F) until a skewer or sharp knife comes out clean. Leave the cakes in the tins for 5 minutes then turn them out onto a wire rack and remove the baking parchment.

I'VE SUGGESTED WEIGHTS AND LAYER NUMBERS FOR MAKING A TWO-TIER VERSION OF THIS CAKE, BUT OF COURSE YOU COULD ADAPT THIS CAKE TO MAKE A ONE-TIER VERSION, OR A LARGER CAKE WITH MORE TIERS BY JUST INCREASING THE BATTER AMOUNT AS NEEDED. SEE BAKING BASICS PAGE 22 FOR INFORMATION ABOUT CALCULATING HOW MUCH BATTER TO MAKE FOR DIFFERENT SIZES OF CAKES.

3. Make the buttercream (see Vanilla Buttercream, page 24) and add a mixture of fresh flower petals to create the base flowerfetti effect. You will also use additional flowers and petals all over the surface of the cake for added flower power!

>>>

4. Split the sponges evenly in half (B), then fill them with buttercream and layer them (see Layering and Filling, page 25) (C and D).

5. Crumb coat the two tiers of cake (see Crumb Coating, page 26) (E), then chill them for 10–15 minutes.

6. Add a second layer of buttercream to coat as neatly as you can (see Second Coating with Buttercream, page 27).

7. Stack the two tiers of cake (see Adding Dowels and Stacking, page 30).

8. Decorate all over the sponges with a flowerfetti effect of petals and small flowers by gently pressing them onto the buttercream (F and G). If you are making a one-tier version of the cake, add the petals and flowers all over the top of the cake, as shown (H).

FAUX FLOWERPOT
ILLUSION CAKES

These adorable mini flowerpot cakes will fool your guests, they look so real! They make a wonderful gift and such a pretty decoration for the table. I've used my chocolate truffle torte recipe for these, which is a lovely fudgy recipe – it is more of a brownie texture than a sponge.

Makes 6

Prep time, 1 hour

Bake time, 40 minutes

Drying time, ideally overnight but at least 4 hours

Ingredients

CHOCOLATE TRUFFLE TORTE CAKE

120g (4¼oz) dark (bittersweet) 70% chocolate chips

150g (5½oz) soft unsalted butter

200g (7oz) light brown sugar

3 eggs, beaten

2 tsp vanilla bean paste or extract

120g (4¼oz) plain (all-purpose) flour

FILLING AND DECORATING

300g (10½oz) chocolate ganache buttercream (see Ganache Cupcakes, page 54)

2 tbsp apricot jam (jelly)

1kg (2lb 4oz) marzipan

Food colourings, I used terracotta and paprika

Icing (confectioner's) sugar for dusting

Edible glue, or agave syrup

Fresh edible flowers and leaves, I've used dahlias, tagetes and calendulas, roses, sweet cicely, lemon verbena and different varieties of sage leaves

Equipment

Stand mixer, electric whisk or bowl and wooden spoon

Cake tin, 18cm (7in) square

Cake leveller or large bread knife

Palette knife

Round cutters, I used a 5cm (2in) diameter one

2 cake smoothers

Sharp knife or ribbon cutter

Marzipan spacers or guide sticks (optional)

Rolling pin

Baking parchment

Scissors

Method

1. Preheat the oven to 160°C (325°F).

2. Melt the chocolate in short bursts in a microwave, or using a bain-marie, and leave to cool.

3. Beat the butter, vanilla and sugar slowly until combined then with your mixer, if using, on fast until light, pale and fluffy.

4. Add the beaten egg a little at a time, on slow, until each bit is incorporated.

5. Pour all the cooled chocolate into your mix, beating all the time.

6. Mix the plain flour in, on slow, until just combined taking care not to over mix or the sponge may become heavy.

>>>

7. Spoon the mixture evenly into the tin, level off and bake for approximately 25–35 minutes.

8. The cake should be slightly under baked, so when you test with a skewer a little cake mix should be stuck to it when you pull it out, paste-y but not glistening wet. The cake should be well risen, but still wobble a bit when shaken; the crust will sink back into the cake as it cools. Cool in the tin.

THE SECRET I THINK TO BAKING A DELICIOUS CHOCOLATE CAKE IS TO SLIGHTLY UNDER BAKE, SO IT ISN'T TOO DRY.

9. Split the cake in half through the middle (A) and fill generously with chocolate ganache buttercream, then press the top crust back on.

10. Cut out little rounds of cake (B) and pop them onto baking parchment (C). Save the off-cuts as they make perfect cake pops, and also we'll use these leftovers for decorating as 'soil'.

11. Add a little water to the jam, and heat it until it boils. Brush each cake all over with jam to make sticky (D).

12. Colour the marzipan a terracotta shade by kneading in food colouring. Roll out the marzipan to approximately 4 or 5mm (¼in) thick (guide sticks or marzipan spacers are useful) (E). Cut little squares of marzipan that are large enough to cover the top and sides of the cake circles.

13. Gently press the marzipan over the cakes with your palms (F) and trim off the excess (a slightly larger round cutter is helpful (G) or use a sharp knife). Save the excess and re-roll for the rest of the cakes and for the edging.

14. Add some icing sugar to your work surface, and with the cut side down, begin forming the pot shapes. Using cake smoothers, press the marzipan onto each cake, holding them at an angle to form slightly A-line shapes, so they look more pot-like (H). Press the bases flat with the smoothers. Leave the pots to dry, ideally overnight but for at least a few hours, so they hold their shape when inverted (I).

15. To finish, turn the pots over so the cut side is upward. Roll out the marzipan and either with a ribbon cutting wheel or sharp knife, cut strips of approximately 2cm (¾in) width and long enough to wrap around the tops. Brush the strips with edible glue and attach around the top of each cake (J), and use scissors to trim off any excess.

16. Spread over some more chocolate frosting to the top of each pot (K), crumble the 'earth' (leftover off-cuts of sponge) over them for soil (L).

THIS RECIPE HAS A GOOD SHELF LIFE OF UP TO TWO WEEKS IF KEPT IN A COOL DRY PLACE, SO YOU CAN MAKE THESE FLOWERPOTS AHEAD, AND DRESS WITH FRESH FLOWERS WHEN READY TO SERVE.

17. Decorate with gorgeous fresh flowers and leaves of your choice, I went for a yellow and orange colour scheme and used a mix of dahlias, tagetes, roses, calendulas, sweet cicely, lemon verbena and sage leaves.

ORANGE AND ALMOND 'TOUCH OF FROSTING' CAKE

A gorgeous wedding cake I made for my friend Louise Roe, which was featured in *Martha Stewart Weddings*, inspires this creation. It's a delicious fairly dense cake, which isn't too sickly sweet – more of a pudding or dessert than a standard sponge.

Serves 70-80 small portions

Prep time, 2½-3 hours

Bake times, 45-50 minutes for 25cm (10in) tier, 40-45 minutes for 18cm (7in) tier and 30 minutes for 10cm (4in) tier

Ingredients

CAKE

8 large oranges, approximately 250-275g (8¾-9¾oz) each

26 free-range eggs

650g (1lb 7oz) polenta

650g (1lb 7oz) ground almonds

1075g (2lb 6¾oz) golden caster (superfine) sugar

3 heaped tbsp finely chopped fresh rosemary leaves

30g (1oz) baking powder

ORANGE DRIZZLE

300g (10½oz) caster (superfine) sugar

2 tbsp orange blossom water

1 tsp finely chopped fresh rosemary leaves

Grated zest of 3 oranges

CREAM CHEESE ORANGE FROSTING

750g (1lb 10oz) soft unsalted butter

1.5kg (3lb 5oz) icing (confectioner's) sugar

200g (7oz) cream cheese at room temperature

Zest of 2 large oranges

Fresh edible flowers of your choice, I've used calendulas, dahlias and alyssum

Handful of kumquats

Several large fresh rosemary sprigs

Equipment

Round cake tins, 25cm (10in), 18cm (7in) and 10cm (4in) diameter

Baking parchment

Cake tester or skewer

Palette knives, large and small

Thin cake boards, 2.5cm (1in) smaller in diameter than the cake tin sizes

Method

1. Grease and line the bases and sides of the cake tins with baking parchment. Put the whole oranges in a large pan or couple of large pans of water, bring to the boil and simmer for 1 hour, until soft. Remove, cool, then halve and discard any seeds/pips.

IT WOULD BE LOVELY TO USE BLOOD ORANGES IF THEY ARE IN SEASON AS A SWITCH FOR REGULAR ORANGES.

>>>

A   B   C   D

E   F   G

2. Preheat the oven to 170°C (335°F). Whizz the orange halves (with the skin) to a purée in a food processor and place in a large bowl. Beat in the eggs.

THE AMOUNTS IN THIS RECIPE ARE THE CORRECT FOR THREE TIERS, 25CM (10IN), 18CM (7IN) AND 10CM (4IN) IN DIAMETER, EACH ONE CONSTRUCTED WITH THREE CAKE LAYERS PER TIER. THIS IS A LOT OF CAKE BATTER, SO YOU MAY WISH TO DEAL WITH IT IN SMALLER BATCHES. CAKES CAN BE BAKED AND FROZEN IN ADVANCE IF YOU WISH AND KEEP WELL FOR UP TO A MONTH.

3. Mix the polenta, almonds, baking powder, sugar and rosemary in a large bowl to evenly mix and distribute the baking powder. Add this to the wet mix.

4. Pour the batter into the tins to the weights stated below (if you only have one tin of each size you can do this in batches) and bake for the times given on page 100, these vary as the smaller cakes will cook more quickly than the larger ones. The cakes should be risen and golden and a cake tester or skewer should come out clean when testing the centre of the cake for doneness. Get your orange drizzle ready whilst the cakes are baking.

I WEIGHED THE BATTER ACCURATELY INTO THE TINS IN ORDER TO KEEP THE CAKE LAYERS OF A SIMILAR HEIGHT. THE WEIGHT OF BATTER FOR THE TINS PER LAYER IS AS FOLLOWS:

» 25CM (10IN) ROUND TIN, THREE LAYERS, EACH WEIGHING 1.2KG (2LB 10½OZ)

» 18CM (7IN) ROUND TIN, THREE LAYERS, EACH WEIGHING 575G (1LB 4½OZ)

» 10CM (4IN) ROUND TIN, THREE LAYERS, EACH WEIGHING 200G (7OZ) .

5. For the drizzle, dissolve the sugar in 100ml (3½fl oz) hot water in a pan. Boil for 5 minutes but don't let it colour. Remove from the heat and cool briefly. Add the orange blossom water, rosemary and zest.

6. Cool the cakes in the tins for 5 minutes, then turn out, pierce with a skewer in several places and brush all over liberally with the drizzle.

7. Use a thin board under each tier that is 2.5cm (1in) smaller than the sponges. This is so the boards do not show through, as the frosting is only a very thin, partially scraped-off layer. Stick the bottom cake of each tier to its cake board with a dollop of frosting (A).

8. Your sponges may need a little trimming to make them all a similar height, although this is a rustic cake so it works well if the heights vary a little. Just layer the sponges together with a generous amount of frosting between each one (B and C), and crumb coat each cake tier (see Crumb Coating, page 26), scraping off the excess frosting and getting the outer surface as neat as possible (D and E). Once all the sponges are coated, use cake dowels in the base and middle tier for support (see Adding Dowels and Stacking, page 30), sticking them together with a little more frosting.

9. If there are any gaps around the joins, add a touch of frosting over these with a small palette knife, or from a piping bag, to fill.

10. Adorn with flowers (F), kumquats and rosemary (G).

BUTTERCREAM CACTUS GARDEN CAKE

I've created this play-on-nature cake with cacti made from Rice Krispie treat. It's a really quick and easy way to make lightweight shapes that stand up well and hold their shape, so this cake has a very sculptural look – I love it! I've used tagetes for the colourful accent flowers, so fun!

Serves 16–20

Prep time, 2 hours

Bake time, 1 hour 15 minutes

Chill time, approx 1 hour

Drying time, minimum 4 hours or overnight

Ingredients

1.5kg (3lb 5oz) batter for chocolate truffle torte cake, see Faux Flowerpot Illusion Cakes, page 96

1.5kg (3lb 5oz) vanilla buttercream, see Vanilla Buttercream recipe, page 24

200g (7oz) chocolate ganache, see Ganache Cupcakes, page 54

A variety of green food colourings

125g (4½oz) of Rice Krispie treat, you can use store bought or make your own (see Floral Krispie Cake Topper, page 64)

250g (9oz) crushed biscuits (cookies), any golden biscuit will do, or see Iced Rings, page 36

Tiny tagetes flowers

1.2kg (2lb 10½oz) concrete-grey sugarpaste, I used a small amount of caramel/ivory and liquorice food colourings

Icing (confectioner's) sugar for dusting

2 tbsp apricot jam (jelly)

2 tbsp white royal icing in a piping bag fitted with a no. 2 round nozzle

Chocolate pebbles (optional)

Food colouring, I used a few different green shades (spruce, mint, and party and eucalyptus for the blue-tinged cactus)

Equipment

Cocktail sticks (toothpicks) or larger wooden skewers

Piping bags

Piping nozzles, I used Wilton nozzles 352, 21, 2, 199 and 47

Rolling pin

Guide sticks/marzipan spacers (optional)

Sharp knife

Cake leveller or large bread knife

Large oven-proof bowl for baking in, either ceramic, glass or metal

Method

1. For this cake, I've used the chocolate truffle torte cake, see Faux Flowerpot Illusion Cakes, page 96. I took the quantities given in that recipe and doubled them to get 1.5kg (3lb 5oz) for this cake.

》》》

A

B

D

C

2. Instead of a cake tin, I baked it in a large metal mixing bowl. I used one with a 3ltr (5¼ pint) capacity, but didn't fill the whole way, I just wanted a nice shallow bowl-shaped cake to make into my planter. The initial baking time was 1 hour 15 minutes at 160°C (325°F), but then I turned the temperature down to 140°C (275°F) for the final 30 minutes.

> YOU CAN USE ANY SPONGE RECIPE YOU WISH IN A BOWL SHAPE, OR PERHAPS YOU COULD DO A SQUARE AS YOU OFTEN GET THOSE STONE PLANTERS, WHICH COME IN ALL SHAPES AND SIZES.

3. Leave the cake to cool in the bowl for 10 minutes, then turn it out on a wire rack to cool completely.

4. Begin by adding the chocolate ganache to 300g (10½oz) of the buttercream to make the filling for the bowl. Split the cake in half, sandwich it with the ganache and buttercream frosting, and crumb coat the surface (see Crumb Coating, page 26). Chill in the fridge for 30 minutes to an hour.

5. Brush over the sponge with apricot jam, then roll out the concrete-grey sugarpaste and smooth it over the cake with your hands. Trim off the excess and use a cake smoother to go around the edge to make neat; place the cake on some baking parchment and leave it to set for at least 4 hours, but ideally overnight.

6. When the bowl is set, turn it over (A and B). Add an additional strip of grey sugarpaste if you need to fill the edges or make the surface level, or use buttercream to do this if you prefer. Add a thin layer of plain buttercream to the top (C), sprinkle with the crushed biscuit 'sand' to cover the top of the bowl (D).

> THIS CAKE IS FILLED AND COVERED IN SUGARPASTE IN THE SAME WAY AS THE FAUX FLOWERPOT ILLUSION CAKES ON PAGE 96 (EXCEPT THAT THEY ARE COVERED IN MARZIPAN), WHERE YOU CAN SEE STEP-BY-STEP PHOTOGRAPHS OF THE PROCESS.

7. For the cacti, colour the remaining buttercream in various shades of green and load up your piping bags, attaching a mix of star and leaf nozzles.

> YOU CAN USE MANY TYPES OF NOZZLES TO GET THE CACTI EFFECTS, HAVE A PLAY ABOUT PIPING SOME TEST SAMPLES ONTO A WORK SURFACE TO TRY OUT EFFECTS.

8. Create structures for the cacti by moulding Rice Krispie treat and place on the cake (E). Use skewers to support the taller ones and give you something to attach them to the bowl cake (F).

9. Pipe over the structures in vertical lines from top to bottom for the taller cacti (G), adding off-shoots in places to make little cactus arms (H).

10. For the round stubby spikey cactus, use an open star nozzle and pipe large spikes all over the surface of a round Rice Krispie ball.

11. For the final details on the plants, add some white dots of royal icing wherever you wish (I), and of course add the little bright coloured tagetes for the cacti flowers by pressing gently onto the icing (J).

12. Fill any gaps with smaller cacti by simply piping plain buttercream to make little ones (K).

13. Add a few chocolate pebbles here and there in the biscuit sand, if using (L).

THIS CAKE IS BEST EATEN WITHIN TWO DAYS, HOWEVER THE SPONGE WILL LAST WELL FOR UP TO TWO WEEKS SO YOU CAN REMOVE THE CACTI AND RESERVE THE CAKE FOR SLICING LATER, OR FREEZE FOR UP TO ONE MONTH.

BUTTERFLY WILDFLOWER MEADOW CAKE

This pretty cake is so easy, as nature has done all the work! Adding gorgeous pressed flowers works really well on a flat iced cake, as they easily glue onto the surface. I've created a few edible butterflies to add some pretty drama – it looks like a real floral scene and would be perfect for a wedding.

A

Serves 80–100 small portions

Prep time, approx 5 hours

Drying time, overnight

Ingredients

Four-tier vanilla sponge cake, filled, covered with ivory sugarpaste and stacked, with round tiers of 10cm (4in), 15cm (6in), 20cm (8in) and 25cm (10in) diameter

3.5kg (7lb 10oz) ivory sugarpaste to cover all four tiers

10g (¼oz) royal icing, for sticking the butterfly wings and bodies

2 tbsp black royal icing

Pressed flowers and leaves, I used violas, pansies, sweet cicely, flowering mint leaves, lavender, roses and bellis daisies

Equipment

10mm ivory ribbon

Printed edible sheets of butterflies (see note on page 110)

Green edible food dusts with melted cocoa butter or coconut oil, and/or green edible-ink pens

Paintbrushes, selection of sizes

Edible-ink pens, in a selection of colours, Rainbow Dust ones are really good

Edible glue and paintbrush

Small sharp scissors

Cocktail sticks (toothpicks)

Turnßtable (optional)

Piping bag

Chopsticks or similar, for supporting the butterfly wings whilst they dry

Method

1. To make your cakes, fill them, crumb coat and cover them in sugarpaste, then stack them, see Very Vanilla Sponge Recipe, page 22 and Vanilla Buttercream recipe, page 24, then Preparing a Cake, page 25. You can, of course, chose any flavour of cake you wish, in any size. A guide to how much sugarpaste you will need is also given on page 28. Once you have created your cake, you are ready to begin adding flowers and butterflies.

2. First, make the butterflies by carefully cutting out the butterfly wings and removing the backing from the edible paper (A).

>>>

FOR THE BUTTERFLIES, I ASKED MY DAUGHTER LYDIA TO MAKE SOME ON HER COMPUTER AS SHE IS A GRAPHICS STUDENT. I'M NOT GREAT AT TECHNICAL THINGS LIKE THAT! THE BUTTERFLIES ARE AT THE BACK OF THE BOOK (SEE TEMPLATES, PAGE 138) SO YOU CAN SCAN THEM AND PRINT THEM OUT ON EDIBLE PAPER, OR OF COURSE, YOU COULD USE PHOTOS YOU'VE TAKEN OR FOUND YOURSELF. I HAVE AN EDIBLE-INK PRINTER, BUT ANOTHER OPTION IS TO SEND YOUR IMAGES TO ONE OF THE MANY PLACES THAT WILL PRINT AND POST THEM BACK TO YOU VERY QUICKLY. I LOVE MIXING PRINTING AND ICING IN THIS CLEVER WAY, BUT OF COURSE, IF YOU WISH YOU COULD EVEN MAKE BUTTERFLIES FROM SUGAR.

3. Use some royal icing, with soft peak consistency, and a small paintbrush to coat the back of each wing, place over a chopstick or similar to set dry (B). These take a few hours to dry, so you might want to do them the day before.

4. Use edible glue on the small pressed flowers to adhere them to the cake surface (C). Some larger, heavier blooms like the pressed roses, may require a dab of royal icing to help them stick. I like to start around the front and build up the pattern. I've done this in broken rings around the cake, so there are moving bands of different height flowers that look like they have grown out from the base of each cake tier. Add the larger blooms, smoothing them with a soft paintbrush if necessary (D), then fill in any gaps with smaller ones.

5. To add the stems and greenery for the flowers, you can either use a small paintbrush and an edible paint made up using green edible food dusts and melted cocoa butter or coconut oil, or you can use edible-ink pens if you prefer. The painted version looks a little more realistic. I start by drawing with an edible-ink pen, then I go over with a brush and dust colours to enhance and add details. See the flower stems painted on the Pressed Flower Faux Frames on page 122 for further examples. You can combine both methods by using pens for the very thin stems then more elaborately painted stems for the larger blooms (E).

6. To add the butterflies, pipe tiny bodies of black royal icing, with a stiff peak consistency, using a small round nozzle, no.2 size or snip a hole in your piping bag. Make the butterfly bodies by piping little beads in a row (F).

G

I

H

7. Add a blob of stiff white royal icing next to the piped butterfly body on each side to support and stick each butterfly wing (G).

8. Place the wings on the cake, pushing them into the body (H). You might find you need a cocktail stick to support the wings while they dry, depending on the angle you wish them to sit at (I). The supports can be removed once the wings have set hard.

9. Leave the decoration to dry and then cover the joins by attaching lengths of thin ivory ribbon (or any colour you choose) to finish off the cake (J).

J

LEMON COOKIE
MONOGRAM CAKE

This beautiful summery cookie cake is so versatile, you could make it in any combination of flavours or colour schemes. Perfect for a birthday, made in the shape of a number, this would be equally lovely as an alternative to a wedding cake, with the bride and groom's initials together with an '&'.

A

B

C

Serves 12-16

Prep time, 1-1½ hours

Bake time, 15-20 minutes per cookie

Ingredients

1.6kg (3lb 8oz) cookie dough, see Iced Rings on page 36, with zest of 3 lemons added

600ml (1 pint) double (heavy) cream

50g (1¾oz) icing (confectioner's) sugar

2 tbsp elderflower cordial, see recipe on page 16 (optional)

Zest of 1 lemon

Flour for dusting

Edible flowers of your choice, I used carnations, dianthus, calendulas, tagetes, rose petals, sunflowers and candytuft

Other decorations (optional), I used physalis, edible gold leaf, lemon meringue kisses and macarons

Equipment

Template, see page 139

Piping bag with a large round nozzle or snipped 1cm (½in) hole

Baking tray/s and baking parchment

Sharp knife

Rolling pin

Guide sticks/marzipan spacers (optional)

Method

1. First make the cookie dough, see Iced Rings, page 36 for recipe, but double the quantities and add lemon zest for flavour. Roll out the cookie dough onto a floured surface until it is approximately 1cm (½in) thick. Cut it into three and transfer the dough onto the baking tray/s (A).

2. Roll the dough out to cover the tray until it is about 4-5mm (¼in) thick, then using the template cut around to create three letters (B). I often bake at least one spare just in case of breakage. Lift away the excess dough from the tray. You can make a template of any size or shape by printing copyright-free letters or numbers from the internet, but we have supplied the template for this 'R' cake on page 139 for you to trace around.

≫≫

I WOULD LOVE TO BAKE A WHOLE WORD OR MESSAGE USING SEVERAL COOKIE CAKES AND HAVE THEM LINED UP ON A TABLE FOR A LARGER CELEBRATION OR GATHERING, IT WOULD LOOK VERY IMPRESSIVE!

3. If you want your cookies to be extra neat and even, it is a good idea to trim them part way through the baking as they will slightly spread/expand. After 10 or so minutes, once the dough is firm but not completely cooked, remove each one from the oven and place the template on the dough again. Carefully re-trim the cookies so that the letter is neat and exactly like the template. Take care as it will be hot, and try not to press down on the card template. Continue baking – in total bake for 15–20 minutes until golden and firm to the touch. Leave to cool completely on the trays (C).

4. Next make the chantilly cream filling. Whisk the cream, icing sugar and lemon zest and elderflower cordial (if using) together either by hand or with an electric whisk until very soft peaks form. Keep it loose, do not over whip as it will stiffen up as you place it in the piping bag.

5. Once ready, place the cream into a large plastic piping bag with a large round nozzle or use scissors and simply cut a 1cm (½in) hole in the tip of the bag.

I LOVE ELDERFLOWERS, THEY JUST SHOUT OF SUMMER TIME – SUCH A SWEET AND DELICATE FLAVOUR THAT COMBINES BRILLIANTLY WITH LEMON, SO WORKS REALLY WELL IN THIS RECIPE. TO MAKE YOUR OWN ELDERFLOWER CORDIAL SEE THE RECIPE ON PAGE 16, AND ADD IT TO THE CHANTILLY CREAM IN STEP 4 OF THIS PROJECT.

6. Place the base cookie onto your display board or serving platter, then pipe little peaks of cream around the outside edge in rows, filling in the centre as required once you have gone all the way around the edge (D).

7. Place the second cookie on top of the cream layer and repeat the decoration (E and F).

8. Add the third cookie (G) and pipe in the same way (H), then decorate the top cookie with edible flowers, and treats if using (I). I've adorned the top layer with some yellow macarons (see Macarons, page 38, but remove the blackcurrant powder and add a touch of yellow food colouring) (J), lemon meringue kisses (see Meringue Lollies, page 42, but add the zest of one lemon for flavour), edible gold leaf, physalis fruit and loads of pretty edible flowers in shades of yellow and cream. I carefully added edible gold leaf using tweezers too (K). It would of course look amazing purely covered in edible flowers.

ANY EXCESS DOUGH LEFT OVER CAN BE BAKED AS EXTRA COOKIES OR KEPT IN THE FRIDGE FOR TWO DAYS, OR ALTERNATIVELY FROZEN FOR UP TO ONE MONTH.

BOLD BOTANICAL
LEAF CAKE

As well as the natural world, I get loads of inspiration from interiors, fabrics and surfaces, and I have always loved luxury interior designers House of Hackney's bold botanical prints. I think this simple and very graphic look, with a colonial feel, is a gorgeous alternative to more flowery designs.

Serves 45–50

Prep time, 1 hour 30 minutes to 2 hours

Bake time, 15cm (6in) tier 25–30 minutes, 23cm (9in) 30–40 minutes

Ingredients

Two-tier vanilla sponge cake, with round tiers of 15cm (6in) and 23cm (9in) diameter

2.5kg (5lb 8oz) vanilla buttercream

Large edible foliage, I used pineapple sage leaves, Peruvian marigold leaves, purple sweet potato leaves, and optional small accent flowers, I suggest tiny tagetes

Equipment

Cake drums, 15cm (6in) and 23cm (9in) diameter

Piping bag, with small round nozzle or a hole snipped at the tip

Method

1. To make your cakes, fill them, crumb coat and cover them in buttercream, then stack them, see Very Vanilla Sponge Recipe, page 22 (or any sponge recipe you wish) and Vanilla Buttercream recipe, page 24, then Preparing a Cake, page 25. Once the cake is ready you can set it on your chosen base – I used a lovely wooden plate, you can use any stand you wish, or cake board – and then you can start to decorate.

2. Turn a leaf over and, using a piping bag containing a small amount of buttercream with a small nozzle or hole snipped at the tip, pipe a little buttercream around the edge (A), or over the main parts. You don't need to cover the whole leaf, just ensure there is some buttercream spread over all the extremities, to help them stick down.

3. Gently press the leaves onto the cake surface (B), all around the sides and over the top, slotting the leaves together in opposing directions to cover as much of the surface as you can (C). You can break some leaves up if needed, or add an extra part of a leaf on by breaking individual 'fingers' off of other leaves to get the perfect spacing.

FOR THIS CAKE I GOT SOME WONDERFUL LEAVES FROM NURTURED IN NORFOLK. THE PINEAPPLE SAGE LEAVES ARE GORGEOUS AND DO TASTE OF PINEAPPLE!

4. You can use a cake smoother if you wish to gently press the leaves on, so as to avoid finger marks, or just very carefully use your fingers and palms with a delicate touch. Add the tagetes, if using (not shown here).

APPLYING THE DECORATION REALLY ONLY TAKES A SHORT TIME, SO IT IS WORTH DOING IT ON THE DAY OF EATING, I THINK, SO THE LEAVES ARE LOOKING AS LUSH AS POSSIBLE WHEN YOU SERVE THE CAKE.

BRUSHSTROKES AND BLOOMS CAKE

I adore this cake, it's certainly a strong contender for top favourite in this book for me. I love the sculptural pastel shards of chocolate candy, which support the pretty roses as they nestle within. I love the clash of the spikey strokes of chocolate with the delicate soft flowers.

A

B

C

D

Serves 40–50

Prep time, 2 hours

Bake time, 40–45 minutes for each batch of cakes (you need five), I fit three in the oven at once

Ingredients

Vanilla sponge cake, 25cm (10in) in diameter, consisting of five layers, filled with vanilla buttercream and strawberry jam (jelly), and covered with vanilla buttercream

2.5kg (5lb 8oz) vanilla buttercream to fill and cover the cake

600g (1lb 5oz) Wilton Candy Melts, in as many pastel shades as you want, I used white, yellow, pink, light green, navy and purple

Edible flowers of your choice, I used roses

Equipment

25cm (10in) diameter cake tins

Baking parchment or trays

Bain-marie or microwave-proof bowl

Piping bags

Scissors

Large palette knife

Cocktail sticks (toothpicks)

Method

1. To make your cake, fill and layer it, crumb coat and cover it in buttercream, see Very Vanilla Sponge Recipe, page 22 (you will need a total of 5kg (11lb) of batter for this cake) and Vanilla Buttercream recipe, page 24, then Preparing a Cake, page 25. Make sure you reserve some of the buttercream to attach the 'brushstroke' decorations.

I BAKED FIVE LAYERS FOR THIS CAKE, MAKING IT REALLY TALL SO THE BRUSHSTROKE SHARDS COULD BE NICE AND LARGE.

2. To make the brushstrokes heat the Candy Melts carefully in the microwave or over a bain-marie until fully melted, mix up your shades and place the coloured chocolate into piping bags.

3. Use a spoon or a piping bag with a fairly large hole snipped at the tip to dollop mounds of melted chocolate, approximately a generous teaspoon to a tablespoon in quantity, onto baking parchment or trays (A). Vary the sizes to give you different lengths and widths. Then use a large palette knife to swipe gently by holding on the top of the chocolate (B), then sweeping downwards in as long a length as you can, until the chocolate becomes thin at the end and a stroke is formed (C).

I MAKE MY OWN SHADES OF CANDY MELTS BY MIXING THE BRIGHTER COLOURS WITH WHITE ONES TO SOFTEN THE HUES.

4. Leave the brushstrokes to set for 10-15 minutes until they are completely hard, before trying to move them (D).

>>>

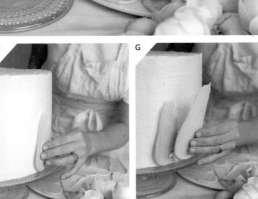

5. Use the brushstrokes to decorate your cake using the remaining buttercream for sticking them onto the top and sides. Pipe a little buttercream onto the cake surface (E), then gently press the brushstroke on (F and G). I went around the base and then created a topper on the top. You can use some cocktail sticks to support the brushstrokes until the buttercream has set, then remove them (H and I).

6. Gently tuck the roses in and around the brushstrokes, and sit them on the top and sides of the cake (J). You may need to add cocktail sticks to support the flowers on the sides of the cake too (K and L).

A WONDERFUL EDIBLE-FLOWER GROWER IN THE UK CALLED JAN BILLINGTON OF MADDOCKS FARM ORGANICS GREW THE ROSES ON THIS CAKE. REALLY ALL THE WORK IN THIS DESIGN IS DONE BY NATURE (AND JAN!) WITH JUST A LITTLE BIT OF MELTING AND SPREADING. IT'S A SIMPLE CAKE TO EXECUTE WELL AS THERE ISN'T MUCH SKILL NEEDED, BUT I THINK YOU AND YOUR GUESTS WILL AGREE, IT LOOKS REALLY SPECTACULAR!

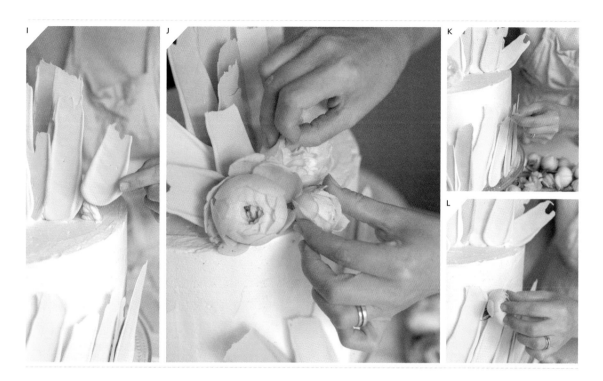

PRESSED FLOWER
FAUX FRAMES

These pretty cakes will be sure to have people looking twice – they look so realistic. I've made frame cakes before, filled with edible butterflies and bugs, so I knew this would look really beautiful if done with pressed flowers. I love the idea of making mini ones to serve as table presents or to box as a gift.

Prep time, 1 hour

Bake time, 50 minutes to 1 hour

Drying time, 4 hours or overnight

Ingredients

25 x 25cm (10 x 10in) chocolate torte sponge

400g (14oz) chocolate ganache buttercream

1.25kg (2lb 12oz) ivory sugarpaste fondant

Icing (confectioner's) sugar for dusting

Food colouring, I used black and brown

Agave syrup or edible glue

Green edible food dusts

Melted coconut oil or cocoa butter

Pressed flowers and leaves of your choice, I used roses, lavender, fennel, Oxford blue tips, sweet cicely, mint flowers, snapdragons, bellis daisies and violas

Equipment

Cake leveller or long bread knife

Baking parchment

Cake board

Sharp knife

Ribbon cutting wheel, or guide stick or similar for cutting frame lengths

Small paintbrush

2 straight edge cake smoothers

Rolling pin

Guide sticks/marzipan spacers (optional)

Palette knife

Paintbrushes

Method

1. You can make these frames in any shape or size, but below I've included steps to make a large rectangle cake from a 25cm (10in) square sponge. I used the chocolate truffle torte recipe (see Faux Flowerpot Illusion Cakes, page 96) for these as it has a good shelf life so they can be made a few days in advance of when you need them. The amount of cake batter in the 25cm (10in) tin weighed 1.3kg (3lb). Bake for 50 minutes to an hour, a cake tester or skewer should come out neither glistening wet or completely clean, but a little paste-y.

>>>

2. To create the frame cake base, split the sponge in half using a cake leveller or long bread knife (A), and generously fill with chocolate ganache buttercream (for recipe see Ganache Cupcakes, page 54).

3. Replace the top of the cake and trim off a length from one side to begin creating the rectangle (B).

4. Add buttercream to one end and add the extra piece of cake to it (C), trimming off the excess bit.

5. Cover the top and sides with buttercream to make one rectangular frosted cake (D). Carefully lift the cake onto a piece of baking parchment and set aside (a cake lifter or thin board is handy to aid moving without breakage).

6. Dust your work surface with icing sugar and roll out the sugarpaste so it is large enough to cover the top and sides of the cake.

GUIDE STICKS ARE HELPFUL FOR KEEPING THE THICKNESS OF THE SUGARPASTE CONSISTENT SO THE PICTURE LOOKS NEAT AND THE FLOWERS STICK FLUSH.

7. Roll the sugarpaste over onto the rolling pin, lift it up and unroll it over the cake (E).

8. Using your palms, press the sugarpaste over the cake to begin shaping it.

9. Use cake smoothers to go all around the sides, pressing the corners to make them nice and sharp, and sticking the sugarpaste flat onto the cake (F). Use a sharp knife to trim away the excess, and keep this in a plastic bag. Leave to dry for at least 4 hours but ideally overnight, so that when you come to add the frames, the cake retains its sharp edges when you cut the frame corners onto the cake.

10. Paint a little agave syrup or edible glue to make a sticky border around the edge of the cake so the frames will adhere (G).

11. To make the frame lengths, knead brown or black food colouring into the remaining sugarpaste to create the wood shade, then dust your work surface with icing sugar and roll out a long shape, big enough to cut a strip as long as the longest side of the cake and wide enough to get a few lengths.

12. Using a ribbon cutter, or something of a suitable width as a guide and sharp knife, create strips of the sugarpaste (H).

13. Lay the first strip on one edge of the cake, keeping it nice and straight. Lay a second piece on to cross over the corner on the first piece (I). Cut at a diagonal angle right through both pieces of icing (J), remove the excess ends and gently sit the two cut pieces together to create the join in one corner. Repeat for the other three corners of the frame.

14. Add a narrower strip of sugarpaste around all four sides of the frame, using the technique described in step 13, to give your picture frame more detail (K).

IF ANY PART OF THE FRAME DOESN'T LOOK QUITE STRAIGHT OR PERFECT YOU CAN GENTLY PRESS WITH A CAKE SMOOTHER TO GET IT REALLY NEAT. DON'T USE YOUR FINGERS OR IT WILL LOOK MESSY! IF YOU WISH YOU CAN ADD ADDITIONAL THINNER STRIPS IN THE SAME WAY TO CREATE A STEPPED FRAME, I'VE DONE A FEW DIFFERENT KINDS FOR MY COLLECTION AND CREATED A WHOLE WALL.

15. To decorate with pressed flowers of your choice, add a little agave syrup or edible glue to the back of your flowers and press them lightly in position (L and M).

16. Add painted stem details if you wish using the green edible food dusts mixed with coconut oil or melted coconut butter (N and O). Some blooms work well without additional painting, depending on the variety.

A LITTLE REJUVENATOR SPIRIT OR VODKA CAN ALSO BE USED WITH EDIBLE FOOD DUSTS TO MIX UP AN EDIBLE PAINT.

BLOUSY BLOOMS
BUNTING CAKE

Oooh I love this one so much! The mix of tiny and larger flowers used in this way to create decorative floral bunting around the cake tiers, is so pretty, and (I'm saying it again) very quick and simple to achieve. It's perfect for weddings, or make a single tier version for a birthday celebration.

Serves 90-100 small portions

Prep time, 4 hours

Bake time, 15cm (6in) tier 20-25 minutes, 20cm (8in) tier 25-30 minutes, 25cm (10in) tier 35-45 minutes

Ingredients

Vanilla sponge cakes, 15cm (6in) diameter, 20cm (8in) diameter and 25cm (10in) diameter, filled and covered with vanilla buttercream

4kg (8lb 13oz) vanilla buttercream to fill and cover

Edible flowers of your choice, I've used a mix of various sizes of tiny tagetes, cornflowers, dianthus, orchids, snapdragons, calendulas, flowering mint, carnations, alyssum, velvet coral, fire feathers, bellis daisies, fuchsias and small roses

Equipment

Cake drums, 15cm (6in), 20cm (8in) and 25cm (10in) diameter

Baking parchment

Scissors

Sharp tool such as a scriber needle/ pin tool or cocktail stick (toothpick)

A little sticky tape

Piping bag filled with additional vanilla buttercream

Small round no.3 nozzle

I FIND THAT LIGHTER SPONGES SUCH AS VANILLA OR LEMON ARE BETTER FOR A PALE BUTTERCREAM FINISH, AS CHOCOLATE ONES MAY SOMETIMES REQUIRE A THIRD COATING OF BUTTERCREAM IF THERE ARE ANY DARK PATCHES OF CAKE SHOWING THROUGH.

Method

1. To make your cake tiers, fill and layer, crumb coat and cover them in buttercream, see Baking Basics, page 22. Each tier is made from three layers of cake. You will need 300g (10½oz) of batter for the cakes in the 15cm (6in) tier, 600g (1lb 5oz) for the 20cm (8in) tier and 1.8kg (4lb) for the 25cm (10in) tier (see Very Vanilla Sponge Recipe, page 22). For the buttercream, see the Vanilla Buttercream recipe, page 24. Then see Preparing a Cake, page 25 for instructions on covering the tiers, but don't stack them yet.

I HAVE CREATED THIS CAKE AS A THREE-TIER STACKED DESIGN, WITH DOUBLE COATED BUTTERCREAM CAKES, BUT ALSO IT COULD BE DONE IN A SINGLE TIER FOR BIRTHDAYS OR OTHER CELEBRATIONS. YOU CAN DO ANY SIZE IN BETWEEN OF COURSE.

2. Make sure your buttercream coatings are dry by leaving the cake tiers to set for a few hours or overnight before marking them out for decorating.

》》》

A   B   C   D

E   F   G

3. Before stacking the tiers, mark out the arcs for the bunting so they look really neat. It's important to do this using the following method, as it's impossible to get it looking perfect by eye. For each tier, cut a length of baking parchment the same width as the height of the tier and long enough to wrap right the way around it. Trim it so the length is exact and it fits perfectly end to end around the cake (A).

4. Fold the baking parchment in half, then fold the half into three, this will give you six sections.

5. Now fold this whole piece in half again and using scissors, cut a U-shape from the middle of the folded edge to the top of the other edge (B). Open out the paper and you will have arcs that will go around the cake perfectly, and be exactly the same size for each section. If you need a deeper U, fold the paper back up again and re-trim until you are happy with the arc. Repeat for the other tiers.

6. Wrap the baking parchment around the cake and secure the join with a little tape, then trace the arcs all around by scoring a line with a sharp tool or cocktail stick (toothpick), so you can see where to place the flowers (C). Do this on all your tiers. Now you can stack the tiers, fill any gaps with buttercream, and then you are ready to add the flowers. You can pipe a trim of small pearls around the bottom of each tier using a piping bag and a no.3 round nozzle (or just snip a small hole in the tip of your piping bag), if you like (D).

7. To affix the flowers, pipe a rough band of buttercream along each arc, spreading this downwards and making it thicker towards the lowest part of the arc (E). Select the tiniest flowers, petals or leaves for the top of the arcs (F) and fill the bunting with different blooms, using the larger ones nearer to the bottom wider part of each arc (G).

THIS CAKE IS BEST DECORATED ON THE DAY YOU WISH TO DISPLAY IT SO THE FLOWERS ARE REALLY FRESH. THEY WILL LAST WELL FOR THE DAY, PLACED IN A COOLER SHADED AREA IN YOUR CHOSEN VENUE. A TENT OR MARQUEE IS FINE FOR THIS DESIGN AS LONG AS YOU PICK THE COOLEST, MOST VENTILATED SPOT. WHEN I MADE IT FOR THIS BOOK, MY CAKE WAS STORED INSIDE AND LOOKED MOSTLY FINE THE SECOND DAY, I JUST HAD TO SWITCH OUT A FEW OF THE FLOWERS FOR NEW ONES FROM THE FRIDGE.

DRIED FLOWERS
WATERCOLOUR CAKE

This ethereal watercolour effect is so effective when paired with the washed-out look you get from dried flowers, which look right at home arranged around the tiers of this cake. Very painterly! I've added tiny flakes of edible gold leaf for an understated touch of sparkle.

A

B

Serves 60–70 small portions

Prep time, 1 hour 30 minutes

Chill time, approx 5–6 hours, or overnight

Ingredients

Two-tier vanilla sponge cake, with round tiers of 15cm (6in) and 23cm (9in) diameter

2.5kg (5lb 8oz) vanilla buttercream to fill and cover the cake

Additional buttercream in different colours, approximately 100g (3½oz) of each, I used gooseberry, dusky pink and pale yellow food colouring pastes

Edible gold leaf

Dried flowers of your choice, I used amaranth, roses, pansies, oregano flowers, bellis daisies, fire feathers, mint flowers, alyssum

Equipment

Cake drums, 15cm (9in) and 23cm (9in)

Palette knives

Side scraper

Cake dowels

Paintbrush

Tweezers or sharp knife

Method

1. To make your cakes, fill them, crumb coat and cover them in buttercream, see Very Vanilla Sponge Recipe, page 22 (or any sponge recipe you wish) and Vanilla Buttercream recipe, page 24, then Preparing a Cake, page 25. Each tier is made from two layers of cake. You will need a total of 350g (12oz) of cake batter to make the 15cm (6in) tier and 850g (1lb 14oz) for the 23cm (9in) tier shown here.

2. Once your cakes have been crumb coated and you have applied the second layer of coating without making it smooth, you are ready to add the watercolour effect. Note that you don't want to stack them until after you have created the colour effect, so get a couple of tablespoons of each of your buttercream colours ready in bowls before adding the second white coating, as this must not dry out before you add the colour.

3. Add dabs of the pastel-coloured buttercream around the side and top of the cake tiers (A).

4. Use the side scraper or a palette knife to sweep all the way around the cake tier in one motion to create the washed-out watercolour effect (B). Neaten off over the top in the same way using a side scraper or a palette knife.

>>>

C

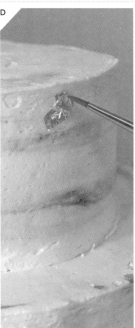

D

E

5. To get a really smooth and neat look, you can go around the cake tier once more with the scraper (C). It does help to have this clean before you start, so run it under a hot tap, shake off the excess water and then sweep round again on the top and sides of the cake. Tidy up any odd little imperfections with a small sharp knife. Repeat this process with the other tier, then leave them both to chill in the fridge for a few hours, or overnight, before stacking.

6. Follow the instructions for stacking cakes in Preparing a Cake (see Adding Dowels and Stacking, page 30), and place on your chosen stand or plate. If you need to fill any gaps between the tiers or at the base, use additional buttercream.

7. Add little flecks of edible gold leaf randomly over the buttercream (D), and then adorn the top edge of the base tier and top tier with dried flowers to finish (E). Perfectly beautiful!

ELECTRO-POP
DRIP CAKE

This cake is the perfect crescendo for this book – it's a drip style cake, which is so easy and very on trend, smothered in a dazzling selection of fresh flowers and fruits. I've also added some of the lovely little bakes from earlier in the book. With a showstopper like this, you almost can't over decorate!

Serves 80-100 small portions

Prep time, for icing and adding drips, 3 hours

Bake time, 10cm (4in) tier 20 minutes, 15cm (6in) tier 20-25 minutes, 20cm (8in) tier 25-30 minutes, 25cm (10in) tier 30-40 minutes

Chill time, at least 6 hours or overnight

Ingredients

Four-tier vanilla sponge cake, with round tiers of 10cm (4in), 15cm (6in), 20cm (8in) and 25cm (10in) diameter

2.5kg (5lb 8oz) vanilla buttercream

Jam (jelly) or curd of your choice

300g (10½oz) buttercream for ombre effect

Food colouring, I used dusky pink and claret

40g (1½oz) good-quality dark (bittersweet) chocolate

Edible flowers of your choice, I used paradise flowers

OTHER OPTIONAL DECORATIONS

Redcurrants

Cherries

Edible glitter

Meringue Lollies and kisses (see page 42)

Dried Flowers Chocolate Bark (see page 48)

Macarons (see page 38)

Equipment

Cake drums the same size as your cake tiers

Additional cake boards, 5-7.5cm (2-3in) larger than each cake tier

Turntable (optional)

Palette knives

Side scraper

Small sharp knife

Cake dowels

Edible-ink pen for marking dowels

Hacksaw or scissors depending on the type of cake dowels you are using

Bain-marie or microwave-proof bowl

Method

1. To make your cake tiers, fill and layer, crumb coat and cover them in buttercream, see Baking Basics. Each tier is made from two layers of cake. You will need a total of 4.7kg (10lb 4oz) of batter for the cake shown here (see Very Vanilla Sponge Recipe, page 22). For the buttercream, see the Vanilla Buttercream recipe, page 24. Then see Preparing a Cake, page 25, for instructions on covering the tiers, but don't stack them yet.

TO MAKE THIS FOUR-TIER CAKE, I USED THE FOLLOWING AMOUNTS OF BATTER:

» 10CM (4IN) ROUND CAKE SPONGES, TWO LAYERS, 175G (6OZ) BATTER IN EACH CAKE TIN

» 15CM (6IN) ROUND CAKE SPONGES, TWO LAYERS, 350G (12OZ) BATTER IN EACH CAKE TIN

» 20CM (8IN) ROUND CAKE SPONGES, TWO LAYERS, 600G (1LB 5OZ) BATTER IN EACH CAKE TIN

» 25CM (10IN) ROUND CAKE SPONGES, TWO LAYERS, 1.2KG (2LB 10½OZ) BATTER IN EACH CAKE TIN

NOTE THAT IF YOU ARE USING OTHER TREATS, INCLUDING SMALLER BAKES, TO DECORATE THIS CAKE, YOU WILL NEED TO ALLOW TIME TO MAKE THESE TOO. ALTERNATIVELY YOU COULD USE STORE-BOUGHT BAKES TO ACCESSORISE, INCLUDING COOKIES, MACARONS AND MERINGUES.

2. Once you have prepared the cake tiers with a second smooth coating of buttercream you can add the ombre bands around them. Begin by colouring approximately 300g (10½oz) of buttercream the darkest shade you want for the bottom tier. Using a palette knife, spread a band of bright pink icing around the bottom third of the largest cake, you can be rough it doesn't need to be a straight line (A and B).

3. Then use the palette knife to push some of the colouring up a little higher around the cake, blending the colour into the white buttercream about half way up the cake tier (C).

I USED DIFFERENT SHADES OF PINK, STARTING WITH THE DARKEST FOR THE BOTTOM TIER AND GETTING LIGHTER UP THE TIERS, TO CREATE AN OMBRE LOOK THAT IS SLIGHTLY DIFFERENT TO THE USUAL AS I JUST USED BANDS ON EACH CAKE, SO IT IS SIMPLER TO DO THAN A FULLY OMBRE TIERED CAKE.

4. Now use the side scraper to swoop around the cake in one motion to give a pretty flat surface with a ring of colourful buttercream around each tier (D). Make this as neat as you can, and finish off the top of the cake. Chill it once you are happy with the coating.

5. For the further tiers, add a few tablespoons of white buttercream to the remaining pink icing in the bowl to lighten it, then go around the second tier in the same way. Repeat, twice more, using more white buttercream so that you are diluting the colour as you work up the tiers onto the smaller cake tiers.

6. Leave all the cakes to chill for at least a few hours, or overnight, before stacking and decorating (see Adding Dowels and Stacking, page 30). You can do this the day before you add the decoration if you wish (E).

7. Now you are ready to decorate! Start by melting the chocolate, either in a bain-marie or in a microwave, and placing it in a plastic piping bag. Adding the chocolate this way will mean you can pipe strategic drips, rather than just pouring it over the cake, so you can get a lovely variety of thin elegant drips in different lengths.

8. Start at the top of the cake, and pipe drips all around the tier by holding your bag at the top and letting the chocolate drip down with gravity (F), holding most of the chocolate back by using your hand to pinch a small amount at the front of the bag so it doesn't come gushing out over the cake.

YOU CAN COAT FRUIT IN ANY NON-TOXIC GLITTER AS LONG AS YOU CAN REMOVE THE FRUIT BEFORE SERVING, AS YOU CAN'T EAT EVEN NON-TOXIC GLITTER. IF YOU WANT EVERYTHING TO BE EDIBLE THEN USE EDIBLE GLITTER LUSTRES – I JUST LOVE A POP OF REAL GLITTER ON SOME CAKES!

9. Pipe chocolate drips neatly around all of the tiers, then using the piping bag, fill in the top surface of the top tier, within the ring of drips. Then fill in the top surfaces of the other three tiers with chocolate (this will fill any small gaps too) (G).

10. Dip some fruits in edible glitter (H), then add them and all the other decorative elements - chocolate bark, flowers, lollies, macarons or whatever you are using - around the cake on the top edges of the tiers and on top of the cake (I and J). You may need to add a little more chocolate to help the decorations on the sides of the cake to stick.

PARADISE FLOWERS ARE PERFECT HERE – THEY ARE LOVELY, LARGE AND SCULPTURAL, SO THEY DON'T GET LOST AMONGST THE OTHER DÉCOR ON THE CAKE.

THIS CAKE IS AN INVITATION TO GO CRAZY AND DECORATE WITH AN ABUNDANCE OF EDIBLE FLOWERS AND EDIBLE FLOWER TREATS. WHAT A WHIMSICAL, CRAZY CAKE! IT LOOKS LIKE IT'S STRAIGHT OUT OF A MAD HATTER'S TEA PARTY, I LOVE THIS FUN CREATION! IT'S A LOVELY IDEA TO CREATE A DESSERT TABLE AND ADD MORE OF THE TREATS THAT FEATURE ON THE CAKE, DOTTED AROUND ON PLATES OR IN GLASSES FOR GUESTS TO FEAST ON.

TEMPLATES

All templates are shown at actual size, but can be enlarged or reduced to suit your own creations. Printable versions can be downloaded from: http://ideas.sewandso.co.uk/patterns.

BUTTERFLY WILDFLOWER MEADOW CAKE TEMPLATE

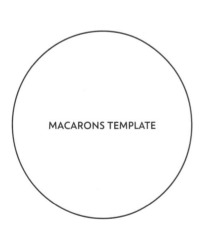

MACARONS TEMPLATE

LEMON COOKIE MONOGRAM CAKE TEMPLATE

139

FLORAL KRISPIE CAKE TOPPER TEMPLATE

ABOUT THE AUTHOR

Juliet Sear is a TV presenter, bestselling author, baking expert and established food stylist. Her reputation as one of the UK's leading cakeologists has seen her work her magic making edible masterpieces for thousands of clients including celebrities such as Prince Harry, Bryan Adams, Kate Moss and Sir Ian McKellen. She regularly appears on ITV's This Morning, and recently worked on the innovative advertising campaign for Channel 4's The Great British Bake Off.

SUPPLIERS

BILLINGTON'S
www.billingtons.co.uk
For unrefined natural sugar

CLARENCE COURT
www.clarencecourt.co.uk
For free-range eggs

GUITTARD
www.guittard.com
For chocolate

THE HOP SHOP
www.hopshop.co.uk
For culinary lavender flowers and lavender essence

KITCHENAID
www.kitchenaid.co.uk
For mixers

MADDOCKS FARM ORGANICS
www.maddocksfarmorganics.co.uk
For organic edible flowers

NIELSEN-MASSEY
nielsenmassey.com
For vanilla and flavourings

NORDICWARE
www.nordicware.com
For beautiful Bundt tins

NURTURED IN NORFOLK
www.nurturedinnorfolk.co.uk
For edible flowers, leaves and herbs

POLKAPANTS
www.polkapants.com
For amazing chefware

RAINBOW DUST
www.rainbowdust.co.uk
For a brilliant selection of edible-ink pens, paint pens, glitters and more

SILIKOMART
www.silikomart.com
For silicone lolly moulds and more

SILVERSPOON
www.silverspoon.co.uk
For sugar and sweetening products

SUGAR SHACK
www.sugarshack.co.uk
For cake boards and bakeware

WILTON
www.wilton.com
For Candy Melts, fondant, nozzles, equipment and loads more

THANKS

Here's my chance to say a great big thank you! So many people have helped bring this book to print, all of whom have made the process such a lovely experience.

I'm so lucky to have so many wonderful friends and food world colleagues to thank who have helped, contributed and supported me through the writing of this book and my work.

To Ame Verso and the brilliant team at F&W, thanks Jason for the lovely shots! And to Sarah Rowntree, Jane Trollope, Anna Wade and Sam Staddon, I love the book, thank you!

Massive family love to Simon for everything and to our three lovely beings, George, Lydia and Ruby #imdoingitforus – couldn't do it without you! Nanny Lydia thanks for always being there to help me and save my headaches and to the kindest Granddad George, squashy bonjer!

To Jen and Jane my wonderful literary agents at GMC, thanks for everything! To team Wexu, my lovely Lucy Chaloner and Ben Hansen, dream team!

Huge thanks to Lola Brandelli my superstar assistant and flavour queen, you are ace. Thanks for helping to make this book as tasty as it is and being an all round champion. Team Cake Club! Rosie Shorten, not only my longest team member but also a wonderful friend, thanks for everything you do, and your famous hand! Dan O Malley my YouTube partner, matey, and legend.

To Jan Billington, you are an inspirational organic flower farmer. Thank you for the stunning flowers (particularly those roses on the brushstrokes cake, so divine!) and welcoming us to Maddocks Farm Organics to shoot.

Also Alan, Sue, Athena, Daisy and the team at Nurtured in Norfolk flower farm. Thank you for growing such beautiful blooms featured in the book and for all your help.

To gorgeous Antonella Bonetti, who kindly allowed us to shoot in the stunning flower garden at Babington House, big kisses, thank you so much!

Rosana McPhee my wonderful exuberant and fabulous agent from Style Department, thank you!

Big love to Natalie Bloxham and the team at This Morning, I love coming on the show and really appreciate your support, it's such fun too!

Big love to Emma Hart, the kindest and cleverest bean, my girlcrush! You and your team at PushPR are truly wonderous, thanks for your endless support.

Billington's babe Leynah Bruce (I love you!) and brilliant team at Silverspoon and bakingmad.com for being my partners in cakey crime since back in the day and shout out especially to Matt Nielsen and the delicious team at Nielsen-Massey.

Thank you Stine Dulong, ceramicist extraordinaire from Skandihus, for many of the incredible props - I didn't want to give them back! And Maxine Thompson, friend and founder of PolkaPants, thank you for the gorgeous camomile print pants, perfect for wearing when baking with flowers or everyday. To my lovely Donna McCulloch AKA superstylish Sulkydollstyling and the fab team at Baukjen thank you so much for the fashion support, to die for!

Lastly to some work allies who are also good friends and I've been lucky enough to collaborate with... Marcus Findlay and team Nordicware - the best Bundt tins and loads more! Thanks to Louise Sansom my FAB friend you are ace, and to team KitchenAid. To Adrian and Emma and the team at Clarence Court including the hens, you're good eggs! Guittard chocolate heroes, so delicious thank you for making such incredible chocolate! Thanks to Claire Stone and the Wilton worldwide team who inspired me originally to get into cake decorating!

And last but by no means least, thanks to you dear reader for buying my book! I hope you love reading and creating from it as much as I did, please share your creations with me.

#botanicalbaking

INDEX

PHOTO CREDITS
The publishers wish to thank Athena Nichols of Nurtured in Norfolk for permission to use the following photographs in this book: cucumber flower, dianthus, orchid, Oxford blue tip, pansy, paradise flower, rosemary, sweet cicely, tagetes and velvet coral on pages 12–15. These images are copyright Athena Nichols, Nurtured in Norfolk.

A SEWANDSO BOOK
© F&W Media International, Ltd 2019

SewandSo is an imprint of F&W Media International, Ltd
Pynes Hill Court, Pynes Hill, Exeter, EX2 5AZ, UK

F&W Media International, Ltd is a subsidiary of F+W Media, Inc
10151 Carver Road, Suite #200, Blue Ash, OH 45242, USA

Text and Designs © Juliet Sear 2019
Layout and Photography © F&W Media International, Ltd 2019

First published in the UK and USA in 2019

A catalogue record for this book is available from the British Library.

ISBN-13: 978-1-4463-0739-7 hardback
SRN: R9974 hardback

ISBN-13: 978-1-4463-7789-5 PDF
SRN: Q0209 PDF

ISBN-13: 978-1-4463-7788-8 EPUB
SRN: Q0208 EPUB

Printed in Slovenia for:
F&W Media International, Ltd
Pynes Hill Court, Pynes Hill, Exeter, EX2 5AZ, UK

10 9 8 7 6 5 4 3 2 1

Content Director: Ame Verso
Photographer: Jason Jenkins
Managing Editor: Jeni Hennah
Project Editor: Jane Trollope
Proofreader: Cheryl Brown
Design Manager: Anna Wade
Design and Art Direction: Sarah Rowntree and Sam Staddon
Production Manager: Beverley Richardson

F&W Media publishes high quality books on a wide range of subjects.
For more great book ideas visit: www.sewandso.co.uk

Layout of the digital edition of this book may vary depending on reader hardware and display settings.